New Life

*Best of live
is love*

Lisa

LISA SONTGERATH

ISBN 978-1-64299-639-5 (paperback)
ISBN 978-1-64299-640-1 (digital)

Christian Faith Publishing, Inc.
832 Park Avenue
Meadville, PA 16335
www.christianfaithpublishing.com

Printed in the United States of America

ACKNOWLEDGEMENT

I feel blessed being surrounded by friends that called as it seemed the right times when I felt alone and lonely.

Like folks from the writers and books club, the gifted Ann Duncan sending me poems that inspire and awakens thoughts and imagination, not to forget my dear artistic friend Hilda Schmied appearing out of the blue with a stroke of her art on paper or canvas.

Kudos and thanks to my family, son David and wife Julie, daughter Sarah, their children and grandchildren for their unending support.

I love you all.

FOREWORD

Since the war in Iraq and Afghanistan began in 2003 the number of veteran has grown to one million. That is not counting the daily attempted suicides and actual suicides that are happening. These men and women have been deployed two and three times before they came home wounded and marked forever... A Veteran . . .

The ongoing question for society as a whole what is the purpose of this brutal mangling of human lives? What are the benefits? Safety, security from the enemy;? We did not have any enemy's until the west invaded these countries with the lies of having nuclear weapons.

Now that we know these statement to be untrue, all those young men, women, fathers, and mothers are enlisted to clean up an ongoing mess that was created by the government, creating "yet a larger war." The cost of human lives, devastation of cities and villages military men and women to protect is a sham an imitation of good, will an expensive fraud. Veterans live with these horrific memories daily creating mental illness, loneliness in institutions and isolation.

The world is tired of war. The list of anti war organisations are growing by leaps and bounds in the US, United Kingdom, Canada, Germany and across the world.

World peace organisation has the idea of living with the willingness of peacefully trying to understand different cultures addressing human rights by diplomacy to creating the end of all forms of fighting. We lived in peace for about fifty years after WW2

I was a teen in WW2, war did not affect me like it would an adult.

Watching parades of soldiers marching through the city of Cologne, Germany, with music, flags, and salutes impressed me as a young teen. Singing, performing, and climbing fences gave my mother a headache.

At the age of 18 my family finally gave me permission to immigrate to Canada where I could dream of my future.

In 1952 I said my good bye to my country in Bremer –haven; sailing on the SS Columbia for Halifax Canada. It took twelve stormy days and two days by train to Hamilton Ont. My future husband followed me then.

My husband developed PTSD

"Post Traumatic Stress Syndrome" I had noticed strange behavior but…love is blind…as they say. It was a disease not well known at the time and treated with shock treatments. After a year in the mental hospital I signed my husband out to live with the family. The warnings from psychologist and nurses of the danger living with a mentally ill person could not change my mind. My spirit and gut feeling told me different,… no person could get well in mental institutions… I was watching the love exchanges between father and our babies. It was all I needed to determine that I made the right choice. Somehow these good meaning folks explaining the danger did not know of the pain watching the loneliness of a mental ill person.

Severe winter hindered my husband's desire to work; bricklayers were wanted in California and we immigrated to Palm Springs. Jobs were plentiful and the weather pleasing. I continued with my busy schedule of being provider mother and student nurse at the University medical center in Loma Linda and later as an RN. Listening to chronic ill veterans off Ww2 seeking refuge at this wonderful facility. So many were fighting with anger, frustration, loneliness, recurring old and new physical pain. Memories usually ending up with the question what was it all for?. I often had the very same questions.

After a short time of working my husband fell back into hallucinating believing he was Christ. He stopped working and communicating. The children loved daddy and could not understand the changes. Times were hard explaining what had happened to daddy loving his family. He refused all help and became inapproachable and after a while I let him be; and my first love passed away at the age of 50.

I had been writing down pains, hardship, difficulties of soldiers and families created by war, and felt helpless in what to say and do easing off believing that powerlessness life is not worth living. Realizing I could do nothing...nothing...to end the war machine, but I could write about it.

My story is a positive one, because, I also believe that all of us can assist helping our hero veterans to live as good a live as he or she is willing. Sharing our own spirit so they can find their spirit not on veterans day only being applauded and celebrated watching them dressed in uniforms with metals marching through the street only to returning these into the droors for another year. We need to remember that they wear their metals daily not shiny ones but with aches and pain for the rest of their lives. That makes them our hero's

My novel will be on shelfs and in stores around veterans day. All the proceeds from this book will be applied to reconstructive surgery.

Love is all we need Lisa

The real voyage of
discovery consist
not in seeking new
landscapes but in
having new eyes

CHAPTER 1

The hands stroking my cheeks, the soft lips that kept kissing my forehead, man, it all felt so good. I was afraid, if I open my eyes, it would end. There, I heard that familiar voice calling my name I remember from somewhere. I wanted to run after it, but I felt so heavy and so tired.

"George, time to wake up," sounding further and further away. Another time, I was feeling backrubs and soft pillows being pushed against my body and that voice again this time in my ear.

"Hello, son, it's time to wake up, it said."

Why would any rational man want to wake up when just a little while ago I was screaming, running, following Joe, avoiding machine gun fire? W here the hell are you, Joe? If you feel the same sensation as I do, we'll just stay here for a while. The sun so warm on my hands. Was someone holding them? That voice again telling stories "Remember, George?" Nothing made sense.

After awhile, I dared to open my eyes to this teary face that looked at me, saying, "Hey, honey."

"Hey, Mom," I responded, just like always. Nothing more natural, but wait a minute. "Mom! Is that really you, Mom? Oh boy!"

Wait a minute, I thought. *This is unreal. Someone put a straw between my lips and offered me some fluid. What is this? A straw? Who the hell are you?* I tried to get out of bed.

"Here, let me help you. I am Mary, your nurse."

As she removed some pillows, I noticed bandages on my shortened legs that no longer had feet.

"What is this? Oh. My. God," I said, falling back into bed, looking franticly around for my firearms, screaming for Joe. And then I remembered the loud explosion, the dust flying, and the darkness.

"Why had I not been told?" I said, frustrated as all hell, trying to sit up again. "Get away from me. I can do this," I said, pushing hands away. "Don't touch me!" I screamed. Finally, exhaustion hit me, or was it the injection they gave me?

I was looking at a male nurse sitting at the bedside when I woke up again.

"George, how are you feeling after your nap?" he said.

Seeing this well-groomed male looking so comfortable gave my hostile feeling a boost. "Who wants to know?" I gave him the most unkind eye contact I could master.

Very calmly and sympathy in his voice he said, "I am Fred, trying to help you."

"Do what I spit out."

"Keep you from hurting yourself and getting better."

Staring at the ceiling, my mind wildly tried to focus on how this—this pretty boy—could help me. Turning his face to me he said, "George I want to explain to you what happen out there."

"How the holy crap would you know what happened out there?"

"Hold on, George, I cannot imagine the horrific night you had, but I am trying to tell you why you ended up here. So please bear with me.

"Now, let me tell you"—turning on my elbow—"what happened because I know. I was there."

"Please leave me alone or I will call the cops you understand?"

Mom was standing at the end of the bed looking at me.

"Tell me, Mom, tell me it is not true that they cut off my legs."

She came to the side of the bed, holding and rocking me.

"Doctors saved your life, son. Apparently, you had severe blood loss in the field, and infection was the reason for the double amputation just below the knees. Then you were flown to this medical center in Landstuhl, Germany."

"You should be happy to be alive," the nurse Fred said.

"Why don't you shut up? What the hell do you know?" I yelled every four-letter word in the book, refusing to listen to anybody. Noticing a wheelchair in the corner sent me into another fury. "Get that contraption out of this room," I cried and fussed, imagining my life being over forever.

With eyes open wide standing in front of me, Mother just said "George" in a tone that I had never heard coming from her. My head spun, trying to say so many things—above all, how sorry I was for my behaviour. I just cried and moaned, hoping to disappear into nothing.

Memories slowly returned. I was wrestling with my friend Joe who had done night patrol twice in a row.

"Go hang your head for a spell, George. You had a tough day. I'll patrol tonight," Joe said.

"Well then, I'll keep you company," I said.

Another hot night, no wind or moon, we were walking and watching the lights turning out in the compound not far away from us. "It's too hot to walk, and I am to nervous to sit," Joe said.

I feel restless myself. "Do you have some gum, Joe?"

"We better stop talking so loud, George. Here, it's my last stick."

"You are a real friend, Joe."

The mine that exploded in front of my friend and me as we were keeping camp that fateful night had taken my legs and my friend Joe's life. That is the report Mother read to me. I remembered the noise and dust of the explosion surprised both of us.

Calling for Joe's voice, while I was trying to get up telling him, "That was a close one."

"Much too close, George. Where are you, George?

"Here, here is my hand. Don't worry, the boys will be here in a minute," I said. Remembering my buddy's fingers slipping out of my hand, sobbing and begging, asking him not to leave me. "Joe, don't do that. Don't leave me," I said as I heard the gurgle of his last breath. I tried to find the hand that slipped out of mine, blind with tears and fear for Joe, not noticing that both my legs were gone.

I must have lost consciousness because that is all I remembered.

The soft kisses and stroking of hands that I felt during sleep were not a dream. The quiet voices and the peace around me were as real as that disastrous night. The teary face speaking to me was my mother. She arrived shortly after me to Ramstein Airbase, Germany.

So I stared into space in my misery for days—between dreams and short periods of semi-awareness of my surroundings in this sterile looking room, thinking of Joe who was now dead. It should have been me. Joe talked of Ann, his wife, who was expecting their first child. Yes, it should have been me.

I'm so sorry, Joe, that I was not more determined that evening. Oh Joe, I loved you like a brother. Why did you have to die? I at least should have died with you. I wrestled in my sleep, as much as I fought with the folks around me while awake.

No one dared to talk to me other than to say what was necessary. Not even my mother could console me. As far as I was concerned, I should have died with my friend in that forsaken desert that we were protecting. I failed to understand what we were doing in Iraq, so far from home. We were surrounded by sand; no green shrubs or trees far and wide. The heat felt intolerable, even at midnight, especially in our combat suits.

The folks whom we protected did not like American soldiers roaming the streets with machine guns, searching for insurgents. How did we know who was who? They all looked alike; angry and suspicious faces stared at us. In many areas, the insurgents mingled with the people. Constant fear of meeting the enemy, who wanted to blow our heads off, kept our nervous energy going.

Why the hell didn't they blow my head off? I thought. It sure would have been better than suicide, which I was certain to commit the first chance I had. I could not go on living with the heavy burden I would be to my family. I also could not see life without legs, being confined to a wheelchair the rest of my life. I thought of opportunities, but while lying in bed, chances were limited. I buried my face into the pillow and cried some more until sleep gave me rest.

After days of suggestion and begging from my mother, I let the nurses help me sit at the edge of the bed. Looking at my shortened legs wrapped in the bandages, my fury became like a raging fire while watching my stumps in constant motion.

"Mom, Mom, look at me, I can't stop it," I wailed and tried to hold both legs. Someone explained these motions were phantom pain. "How the hell can anybody cut off my legs without asking my consent?" I screamed. "How can this be? How can this be done to me?" I moved franticly to the edge of the bed.

A couple of men in white held me down until the injection took effect, I guessed. Sometime later, a person with a stern face asked whether I was ready to get out of bed. Without waiting for an answer, they lifted me into the wheelchair. Cursing, I sat there. I felt weak and light-headed. I noticed my mother's smile.

"At least you are happy, Mom. Don't you get it? They cut off my legs." Moving my hands up and down my stumps trying to find my legs, I cried. I wiped my tears on the sleeve of my shirt.

"Oh, sweetheart, nobody cut off your legs. The grenade took them." She tried to make me understand.

The attendant invited us to go to the dining room for some food. I felt everyone's eyes on me as my mother tried to fit the wheelchair under the table. Eventually, someone came over to help her.

It was the first time I sat at a table since I couldn't remember when. Resentment and anger made their way into my mind and body. Like a volcano, screams bubbled out of me, blindly looking around for an escape to get out of the wheelchair. *Run, George, run.*

"Hold on, buddy," someone in uniform shouted. "You are not the only one who is hurting here. Open your eyes and look around you. We are all in the same boat," he said.

That I did, look around. I noticed someone was feeding a young guy at the next table. Just like a baby, he opened his mouth and ate. A grown man was being fed. At another table, a person with his eyes covered was being helped. Physical disfigurement all around me. My eyes could not take another tragedy; with my heart aching as it felt to come right out of my chest, I asked to be taken to my room, and there I sat and stared.

My mother was sitting beside me, while I was planning to end my life as soon as possible. Mother was a hurdle; I needed her out of the way. I could not leave her with another trauma. I would request that she not be informed of my suicide.

"Tell me, Mom, where are we? How long have I been here? Is it safe for you to be here?"

"We are in Germany."

"At least we are on peaceful grounds. Why Germany?" I asked. "Why not the USA?"

"This is an American hospital."

The daily battle with dreams, confusion, and physical pain did not get me any closer to my goal of being with my buddy Joe.

The feeling of wrongdoing and weariness was a steady companion. *Sorry. I'm so sorry, Mom, that I did that to you and so many other mothers in Iraq. I killed Mom because I feared for my life. How can I go on living?*

I was helped in and out of bed every day. Each time I awoke, Mother was still beside me; but I noticed her features became more relaxed.

"You had a good sleep, George," she would say. Between tears and choking on words, I asked her to forgive me for the sorrow I caused her. I kept my suicidal thoughts to myself, another big hurdle for my family to overcome. But what else was there for me? How could I erase the harm I had done? How could I make my mother proud of her son?

"I am a cripple, a hobbling invalid for life," I cried out. "It's all over, Mom. Do you understand? It is all over for George. How could it all go so wrong?"

I had a normal childhood, school friends, followed by a typical American college life. Even during college, I thought about my goal of going into the army, learning to discipline myself. During Bible study in my youth, I heard about noble souls, saints contributing to the betterment of mankind. What made me think I could get this in the army, I would never know. I looked at Mother's peaceful expression, her hands in prayer.

"Just get well, son. We will go home. Don't worry about anything."

CHAPTER 2

*T*otally against my will, slowly, I learned how to get around. Like someone being chased, I drove that wheelchair through the halls when anger became uncontrollable. I felt like I would explode into orbit at anytime. I felt rejected and thought I might as well give everyone a reason for disliking me. Whenever I thought about my bleak future being stuck in the wheelchair, the thought of suicide spoke loud and clear, wanting to take my life any way possible.

Hell, what are they nursing me back to do? What will I be for the rest of my life? There was no future as I saw things. Why could no one understand it? Dancing and running around with friends was history. Thinking of ever getting married was questionable. Father Paul had explained that God would not test his children with more than they could handle. He also talked about the stages of grieving, overcoming anger first, before healing could begin. But I did not hear or understand any of it.

What did these people know while they were safe, eating, and drinking when and what they want? How could they understand the fight out there, always watering their body and sweating it out at the same time? We were always on the alert even when not in battle. During battle, we screamed because we needed to hear voices of our buddies—running behind the wheels of a jeep, ending up in a hole for momentary safety, hoping for enough time to have a puff and a few hours' rest. That is the life of my fellow warriors out there.

We were a close bunch; we knew each other's honey's name and showed pictures of children, parents, and home. Omar tried to talk religion and read out of a small Bible. When I saw the rosary beads moving between his fingers, I asked him, "You really believe in Holy Mary?"

"Yes, I do. I call on her when I am afraid, and that is all the time."

"Well, she didn't save her own son from the cross," Bill said.

"That's different. Jesus had to die to fulfill the scriptures," Omar responded.

Those minutes of camaraderie were rare but meaningful for us. I wondered where my buddies were at this time. I wanted to be them at this very moment.

Gee, Joe, I should have persisted to take patrol. Your wife would still have a husband, and you would get to hold your new baby. I tried to control the storm of tears running down my cheeks.

I called on God. "This is me, God. If you are out there, please hear me. I felt empty again. Day in and day out, I felt empty and tired, older and with no interest in life."

CHAPTER 3

One morning, sitting at the edge of my bed cursing another day, I saw an occupied wheelchair standing in the doorway. A man waved his bandaged arm stumps at me. "Good morning, buddy. I am going home today."

The girl standing behind the chair smiled at me and said, "But Daddy will come back for new hands and feet. God needed Daddy's hands for someone else," she explained.

I sat there aghast for I don't know how long. What I just saw was a man without his upper limbs sitting propped between pillows in a wheelchair smiling at me. What I just heard was a girl with shiny black eyes talking about God with unwavering faith. *Is such a thing possible?* I wondered.

Suddenly, I realized I had hands. "I have hands!" I held them up in front of me. "I have hands." I looked at them, examined them, turned them, used them, and they work. *Oh. My. God. God left me my hands.* I fell back in bed, buried my face in my pillow, and cried bitter tears.

Shame and remorse overcame me as I reflected on the picture that had been in the doorway just moments before. The bravery of that soldier telling me that he was going home and being totally dependent on family members opened my eyes. I could not envision living without hands.

Again and again, I was overcome with gratitude. I reexamined my hands and caressed them, which made me realize my blessings. It took an appreciative comrade less fortunate than myself to remind me that the bomb that hit me could have taken my hands too. Someone helped me into my wheelchair, and there I stayed for the rest of the day wrestling with God and myself. "Lord, I am not worthy of my hands you have left me with. With my hands, I can do so many things. How can I make use of them for others?"

My mother watched me doing things for myself that afternoon. She asked me about the strange motion I made with my hands. I told her about of what I had experienced. I noticed her eyes filling with tears as they looked upward. Then she took my face into her hands and kissed me, without saying a word.

"Mom, it's a mystery to me. I have never seen that man before. How and why did he end up at my door?"

"Yes, dear son, God does things in mysterious ways at times, and it is not for us to question."

Later when I wheeled my chair through the corridor slowly, I looked at my hands. I used them for getting around without even thinking about it. I watched what was happening around me and hoped nobody would find out the shame I felt about my previous behavior. No one was to know what was going on inside me. For the first time, I noticed the many soldiers who were at this rehabilitation center for the same reasons I was here. All had been wounded in Iraq.

Cautiously, I waved to groups of men sitting around reminiscing. Frequently, I heard them say, "I never thought I would make it home" or "What a hellhole." Some men just stared into the distance. I heard men speak of the fear they had when it was their turn to patrol at night. I remembered my buddy Joe and I exchanging conditional promises to God if he could get us home again.

The next few days, I felt exhausted trying to remove the guilt and remorse from my brain, exchanging my hostile thoughts with composure and tranquility. Having hands and using them were highlights during these days, realizing I could still use knives and forks. At times, I felt a faint desire to rebuild my faith and hope in God and fellow human beings, but then I remembered life in the trenches and my friends still out there and the nincompoops who sent us there. Those thoughts fired my brain with enough poison to explode. If only I could get rid of those outbursts of hate toward government officials.

Father Paul noticed a change and said one morning, "Let's have it, buddy. What are you fighting?"

I told him what I had experienced over the last two weeks and couldn't get rid of feeling like a heel.

"Well," he said, "the best remedy for this is prayer." So he prayed for me, saying the words that I wanted to tell God but hadn't had the guts to do.

I repeated the words after Father Paul.

"That was not so hard, was it?" he said. "Just believe. Point your hands up, tell him what you want, and trust that he will deliver, buddy. It will be in his time, however, not yours or mine. Remember that. You will be successful, you'll see." Then he left.

I was left curious. If life and success were so easy to reach, why did our politicians and men in power not use prayer to prevent wars? Why is there hunger, death, hate, and greed? I could not understand it.

I sat in my misery for a while, until exhaustion took over and I found sleep. I woke up with the phrase on my mind, *Just believe it.* Hell, I have nothing to lose. With that in mind, I started working on my attitude. I worked on getting rid of my anger and hate by telling the Lord what I felt. Sometimes I screamed and cried at him, "Why do I have to wait? Help me, help me now." The help came not from heaven—rather, a syringe.

CHAPTER 4

*M*other and I walked by the library one afternoon. I disliked the library in my younger years; it meant learning, having to be quiet, and isolation. This time, I looked at books differently—all those rows organized into many categories. Mom wheeled me through an area that read "Psychology, Bibles and Religious Books." She picked two books from the shelf and asked whether there was something I was looking for in particular.

"Yes, Mom. I want to read about how I can regain my faith."

She sat down in a chair opposite, looking at me. She said, "Son, faith, hope, and love is not learned overnight. It's like wanting to lose a hundred pounds of extra weight right now, but it takes determination and time. You must really want to love God and your fellow men. Don't worry, just work at it daily as all Christians have to do."

I was holding two small, old, and tattered books, one by Will J. Derwood and a paperback by Bill Johnston called *The Supernatural Power of a Transformed Mind*. I think that I should find something in either of those books to help my brain. My mother signed them out, and on the way to our room, she mentioned that Derwood was my dad's favourite author and we still have a copy. I ask her if she had read it, and she told me stories of Dad reading to her in the evenings. It was usually at times when the weather was too bad for him to work outside. Then, when he became too ill, she would read his fondest pages to him.

"Will you read some of those to me tonight, Mom?"

"Yes, I will, George."

"Mom, was Dad a praying man?"

"Your dad was the most grateful individual I ever knew. Even when I feared about something, he would not pray for help because your dad never doubted. He thanked the Almighty for taking care long before help came."

Dozing into sleep that night, I thought, *George, you are a lucky man having parents like Mom and Dad.* I felt warm and secure, just like when I was young and biked home in the evening and saw a light burning. I promised myself to stay focused on rebuilding my faith.

Slowly, I mingled with other men and listened to their stories. I noticed so much sadness, yet I heard words of hope or God willing frequently. These bits and pieces combined with watching the dedicated nurses assisting wherever they were able to make their patients comfortable. I watched new comrades come in wounded and mutilated, crying, moaning, or cursing. Then, I was in danger of losing whatever hope I had started to accumulate, making room for hate and a need to retaliate against any authority who wanted this war. But Mom prayed for them too. She said, "Son, they are our leaders, we, the people, voted for them."

There were so many things I could not understand. We sat alone, Mom and I, watching the soft rain gently hit the window when I heard the helicopter bringing new wounded.

"Mom," I asked, "tell me, how can God let all this suffering happen?"

"Son, this is not God's doing. There has been suffering since the beginning of time. Remember, dear, Mary tolerated the greatest suffering when she watched her son Jesus on Golgotha's."

It was all beyond my comprehension.

We were on the second floor. Often, I wheeled my chair close to the glass partition to watch the new soldiers come in one floor below. They were being registered and receiving care. I felt the urge to use my precious hands to touch the new comrades.

Nurse Toni told me that I was not allowed in that area. "When you get better, you can come and greet some of them," she said. "I will make sure to let the other nurses know. One of us will show you where and when. You can help us feed or read to the wounded."

From then on, nurses showed me when and how I could be of help. Some soldiers did not come directly from the war zone but from another hospital to have special procedures done. Being able to help had a positive effect on my attitude, and my perception of knowing their needs helped me gain control. It seemed that my own grief was fading. "Mother read something the other day about forgetting oneself, and healing those in need." Words in one of her favourite books. This feeling was true to what I felt being with my buddies.

When I was tired, I either returned to my room or sat for a spell in the chapel. In this place, I could wrestle with my thoughts and clean the corners of my mind, removing those hostile thoughts that still came to the surface during the day. The dark and quiet of the chapel helped me find words to talk with the Higher Power as tears fell into my lap. After a while, anger and bitterness slowly turned into gratitude as I listened to the organist playing hymns.

As I wheeled myself back into the sunroom, I passed folks talking how happy they felt being on peaceful soil or say "Thank heavens," which swept me up with emotion. These where good feelings, and I wanted more of them. As I spent more time with others, I realized again that my own loss was fading. I did not need my legs for what I was doing. I knew that I was not out of the woods, but I had found strategies to intervene whenever those violent spells got the upper hand.

My thoughts drifted to my friend who now lived without limbs. I wondered how he struggled with his demon power of which I was still trying to gain control. Fear and grief still made me physically ill. I had stomach problems and headaches when I let go of controlling my emotions. Nevertheless, I was learning to feed my sick brain with positive thoughts either from buddies or books.

I read creative thinking is fearless thinking. It is unrestricted, unlimited, but consistently and intelligently directed thinking. *Powerful words, George. Concentrate, George.*

"Fight that resisting mind of yours and accept what is now unconditionally and without reservation. In other words, don't be plagued with emotional negativity for what could or would happen. Decide what you want your mental attitude to be before putting it into action. That is what will get you out of this mud." I found these words and wrote them on a piece of paper so I could memorize them.

Prayers came easier this last while. I asked God to be with my brothers in the field and help Joe's wife, Ann, and to give me courage to focus on what I needed to do.

CHAPTER 5

Whenever I felt the most content, I was wheeled away to have something done to me. I remarked to Garry that for a recuperating guy, I have a lot on my schedule.

"Yes, you are important to us, George," Garry said, tapping me on the shoulder. He wheeled me into the examination room where Dr. Kopp was waiting for me.

I could not help smiling back at him; his face beamed as he smiled from ear to ear. *Oh boy, here comes another pep talk*, I thought.

"I hear great things about you, soldier," Dr. Kopp said while shaking my hand. "You look good. Let's look at those wounds of yours." He helped the nurse to get me in position on the table.

"Trapped again. You leave me no way to escape, Doc. Nice going, checking the flesh of my stumps."

"I am feeling for soft spots, but all feels good and firm," he said.

Listening to those professionals discussing flexion and extensions of the ligaments and muscles did not make much sense to me, but I guessed it had something to do with what I was staring at.

I asked, "Are these contraptions standing against the wall for me?"

"Yes, they just arrived. Those prostheses will get you out of this chair. I think you are ready for measurements and to try them on. What do you say, George?"

We exchanged a long look. After probably having read my mind, he said, "You have come through hard times, and each day you become more and more important to all of us around here."

How can this be possible? I almost shouted at him. I am a cripple. "I will never be able to lead a normal life—go out with buddies, dancing, have a wife and some kids. How important can my life be?" Here I was again, totally out of control.

"Move over," Dr. Kopp demanded. Sitting beside me, he took my hand and told Garry to get some coffee. It was quiet for a while, and then he talked about himself and his mission.

"You know," he said, "I work sixteen to eighteen hours most days, often seven days a week. Rarely do I see my wife and four kids. If it were not for guys like you and the rest of them, I would not have that energy. I love being here among you heroes. When I hear of what you and the others are doing out there in no-man's-land to keep us safe at home, I pray for wisdom and energy to do my best." Looking into my teary eyes, he said, "Yes, George. I am grateful being here and happy to be helping everyone here to recuperate to a life as normal as each of us can have."

He talked about the great advancements in the prosthesis industry. "People are running marathons"—he smiled—"honest. I had a tour at a factory in Sri Lanka, of all places. You may have heard of the tumultuous tsunamis in the area that left so many people in need of artificial limbs. American businessmen, with the help of the government, opened a factory, fabricating devices to help folks lead a fulfilling life."

He squeezed my hand then mentioned how I was angry and devastated.

"We were on the brink of medicating you for depression, but we held off, hoping you would get yourself out of this morose feeling. You know these medications have a lot of side effects you would have to cope with, and we thought you might become suicidal. Therefore, we waited a little longer."

I sat still, wondering if he knew of my thoughts. I had questions, but I could not get a word in; he was full of emotion.

"Your mother was a great help to us," Dr. Kopp continued. "Believe it or not, we are a praying bunch around here, and as you know, your mom is too. Working here with individuals such as you, prayers come in handy. We were on the brink of losing you, George. The blood infection almost won. Experience taught us that when human knowledge does not work, to pick up some wisdom from the Source. The results are usually very good.

"Your best medication is what you are doing—helping and chatting with your comrades, giving hope where only anger and darkness lives. You know all about that, George. You are very effective, I hear. Keep at it. Help us, and we will help you. You see, you were there and understand the men that come to us. Yes, George, you are an important man to us, and in regards to the future, I tell you what, leave it up to the Almighty. He will take care of all you care about because, George, there is nothing but nothing impossible with him.

The phantom pain started to act, and my back was beginning to hurt from sitting without support on the examination table. A pretty nurse suggested for me to lie down. "Now, let us look at the equipment here. Feel these how light they are, George. You know, with these new techniques, most physical repairs are possible. Just look around here, read of other rehab centers on what is being done for guys like you. It is astounding."

Sitting up holding my new legs, I wondered how I could get used to these. But Dr. Kopp kept on preaching, "Plan your new life, having everything you can dream of." My mind ran away from me. I pictured myself being seen wearing these. Swallowing for words, I felt my heart pounding, trying to get off the table. The nurse and Dr. Kopp assisted to get back into my chair.

"What, George, what? Spit it out. I want you to say what you are thinking," Dr. Kopp said.

"OK, if there were no wars, we would not need all these rehab centers in the world."

"You are right, young man, but I am unable to prevent wars."

"I didn't know you were watching me that close," I said to Garry, as he was wheeling me back to my room.

"You know, George, I don't know where that man gets his energy from, honestly. He eats on the run and sleeps very little. His family comes to visit him here in the hospital. Matter of fact, they have an apartment right here. His oldest son, about ten, goes with him when his dad makes his rounds. He looks just like him, very tall for his age and has a ready smile for every one."

CHAPTER 6

The prayers became the medicine for healing my physical and emotional instability. My refusal to have the prostheses measured changed. I watched other men exercising, noticing how many men walked with artificial limbs and tried to keep their frustration under control. An uphill fight for sure, I thought, but with the perseverance and the dedication of the staff with others and me, I inched forward in toward an optimistic way of thinking. The thought of suicide for some time and the pills that I had saved I flushed into the toilet.

I watched wives and lady friends coming and going. The endearments and loving support felt so touching to me. I begged God to help me find a wife with whom I could live a normal life, someone with whom I could have children. More and more I found myself dreaming of a normal life. At times, I thought about the soldier at my door. He opened my eyes to the blessing of having hands I could work with. I prayed for his family to remain courageous. How much affection that family had to have in order to take care of such a crippled individual? I pictured his wife dressing, feeding, and bathing him. Was so much dedication possible?

CHAPTER 7

ntering the chapel one morning, I listened to a beautiful voice accompanied by the organ. Her voice sounded crystal clear. With my eyes closed, I tried to understand the words of the hymn. Father Paul interrupted my peaceful moment.

"What have we got here?" he shouted.

With that, the organist turned and came walking toward me. I was introduced to a smiling young woman. Immediately, that feeling of being a lower-class citizen fell upon me, and I was tongue-tied.

"Why don't you come to the front? I like some company." She gestured her head toward the organ.

"Here I'll help you," Father Paul said, marching down the long hallway with me. I heard him say, "This is George from Oklahoma. He's here with us to recuperate."

I was sitting in the midst of many papers and music books on the floor.

"Nice to meet you, George. My name is Angela," she introduced herself. "I am practicing a song that I will be singing at a concert in two weeks. I don't know my music yet. I'll sing and play it for you. Be honest now, George, and tell me how I sound."

I still had not found my voice, so I motioned with my head.

Sitting in front of the organ and turning her head, she said, smiling at me, "Here it goes. There is someone who loves every sinner, this Jesus, our blessed Redeemer is only a prayer away. He has infinite power and so many things he can do."

There it was again—that deep, profound sensation I could not handle. I turned my chair around and left the chapel. Back in my room, I closed the door and prayed.

"He is only a prayer away," Angela's words rang in my head.

"If so, God, help me to do or say the words you love to hear," I moaned.

I did not see my mother standing behind me, saying, "Let's do it together and pray the Lord's Prayer. With no further talk, she handed me a wet, cold cloth to wipe my face. I fell asleep in my chair.

A few days later, Angela—the organist—sat beside me at lunch. "Remember me?" she smiled.

"Sorry"—I stumbled—"I forgot your name."

"But I did not forget yours, George. You ran away without telling me how I sounded." She searched for my eyes.

God, I felt so inadequate.

Someone came to my help. "Well, what is your name?"

"Angela," she said.

The folks around the table laughed.

I could just stare into those blue, shiny eyes. There was more laughter and clapping of hands. *I had to get out of here*, I thought.

Angela noticed my discomfort and suggested a walk.

"Let's go," I said.

The sunshine felt good. We listened to folks' greetings and small talk, walking along the wide sidewalks or sitting on benches. I realized that I had not been outside for a long time. It looked all so green, and the fresh-cut lawn smell—oh, how good it all felt—I remembered that I always had enjoyed gardening before my soldier life began. *Hell yes, I did have a life*, I thought.

Angela walked quietly beside me. After a while, she wheeled me back to my room. "If you'd like, George, I will walk with you tomorrow."

"Thanks," I said.

Before leaving, she invited me to the concert.

"I will think about it," I answered.

"OK," she replied, and then she was gone.

Will she really come back? I wondered.

Not only did she come back, but she visited me when I was with the therapists.

"It's OK, George, we work with one another. I am a nursing student and am allowed to come and watch how therapists train patients regaining bone strength."

"I don't care. I don't want you to watch me."

"OK, but don't forget the concert."

Angela's interest frightened me. In my heart, I loved it; but how could a beautiful, young woman be interested in me, incapacitated? As I went through the daily exercise routines, Angela's name came up frequently in my thoughts. I realized I was dreaming the unthinkable. At times, the therapist would remind me to focus.

It was hard work to get the quadriceps and hamstrings into shape. Most of the muscles below the belt had become soft due to sitting in the chair. Jim explained how lucky I was to have healthy kneecaps.

"You should not have any problem wearing your prosthesis all day." Jim explained that massaging the kneecaps, practicing getting in and out of bed, and turning from side to side without assistance was hard work.

I was introduced to a psychologist, Dr. Philips.

"I know, George. You are wondering why you are in need of me," she said, shaking my hand. "But there will be times when you do not feel as upbeat as you do now. It is essential for our patients to maintain a positive attitude. You have been here many weeks and have gone through some tough times. Dr. Kopp thought it might be advantageous to have a friend when times are difficult. I am that person, George. Together, we will get rid of any negative thoughts lurking around when you are tired and not feeling up to what Jim wants from you. He expects a lot from his clients."

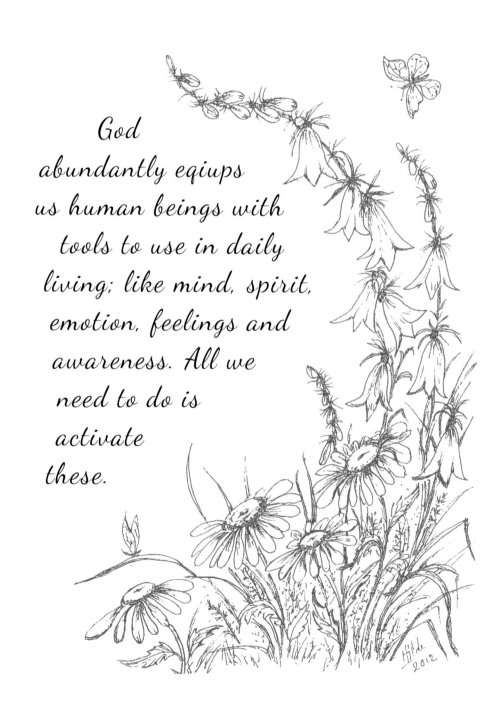

God
abundantly eqiups
us human beings with
tools to use in daily
living; like mind, spirit,
emotion, feelings and
awareness. All we
need to do is
activate
these.

.

CHAPTER 8

One morning, my mother came storming into my room, telling me, "I will become a grandmother soon! Your sister, Margaret, is expecting a baby girl in the fall."

Frankly, I had never seen my mother so excited. Oh, she could be excited seeing the first crop shoot from the earth in springtime; otherwise, she usually walked and talked quietly. I was speechless. Nothing registered for some time.

Right, I thought. *I left my older brother, David; my baby brother, Peter; and sister, Margaret, crying at the train station.* It seemed a life-time ago.

I remembered feeling very important flying by myself to boot camp. I also remembered that, just thirty minutes into the flight, I was hiding my tears feeling alone. *Look at me now, sitting in a wheel-chair feeling helpless like an old man without legs. How in the world will I face my siblings?* I thought of home and family members, the farm, the horses, and Ella my favourite horse. *Will I ever stroke her again? Would she recognize me?*

Remembering that my family and school friends gave me a great going-away party. Some girls had little gifts of knickknacks to be safe; others had given me hugs and kisses and reminders for me to write to them. Karl, my best friend, had tried his dandiest to get a date with my sister. I remembered making up ugly stories about her so that he would lose interest in Margaret. I had it in my mind to find her a boyfriend. She was my only sister, and I had to watch out for her, even though she was older and, yes, much wiser than I in many ways.

But, only a girl, I thought. *Where might Karl be now? Did he sign up for the army or did he go into business with his dad?* He told me at that time that he did not like the latter because his dad was very disciplined and the army was an alternative.

Oh boy. I felt as though I was moving into another world.

While Mom was laying the pictures on the bed, I asked, "How come I haven't heard about any of them?"

"Did you not receive the mail we sent?" Mother asked. "I could not remember having received any mail. Being on active duty, who knows?"

I thought of my little brother, Peter. He was the baby, and I loved him. "Mom, what is Peter going to say about me being an invalid?"

"Don't you worry about what Peter or anyone will say. They can hardly wait for you to come home. Margaret is married to a fine young man. Brad is flying a helicopter."

"Where, Mom? Where is he flying that chopper, Mom? Where the hell is he? Do you know how dangerous that is?" I pictured how we tried to protect these choppers in the field. I felt my body shaking, my stumps jumping up and down completely out of control.

"Hold on, son," Mom alarmingly said, "your imagination is running away with you." She called the nurse, realizing all the news was too much information.

The medication nurse Nancy gave me an intravenous shot. Soon, I relaxed and fell asleep.

It wasn't long 'til I was crawling in the sand, listening to the incoming helicopter trying to land in order to remove our wounded after a stormy fight. Ground forces had to keep them safe from the insurgents trying to shoot the helicopter down. The fear of them succeeding was great, and no one was thinking about their own well-being at the time, just to get the wounded out of danger and the chopper in the air.

Running, watching where the shooting came from, we were busy shooting and screaming. I remembered after each successful mission, we collapsed—sometimes only for minutes—as the sounds from the chopper drifted high in the air, becoming quieter by the second.

After name call, we exchanged thoughts of home, knowing someone was heading for home. Home, that priceless word. The sound of a helicopter usually made us feel homesick and happy at the same time. It was that feeling all soldiers feels when they hear choppers above them in the fields and then watching them becoming smaller as they leave. It meant safety and hope for the wounded. Suddenly, I was there, fighting in that heat, falling down, getting up, and running behind a jeep, trying to protect a chopper.

I woke up tired and wet from exhaustion. Of course, my mother knew nothing of what my alarm was about when she said that her son-in-law flew a helicopter. While I slept, my mother had posted some pictures on the wall. I could not help but look at them as I woke up—schoolmates with whom I ran around, boys with whom I smoked cigarettes behind the barn, my horse Ella. I used to run too when I as a kid and knew I had done something that deserved a spanking.

It was a world that I had left long ago. "So far away." I remembered saying words like *home* or names that popped up when homesickness made my gut turn.

I lost track of time and did not want to sort out my scrambled mind. I heard my mother talking with somebody. I wanted to sleep and not wake up. *God, grant me sleep.*

Dr. Philips came, having been notified of me fighting with hallucinations. I had no interest in anything.

"We have appointments, and they must be met, George. Jim is waiting for you."

Reluctantly, I followed her to the exercise room. On the way, she asked me if I had heard from veteran's administration

"Veteran's administration?" I felt immediately alarmed. "What do I have to do with them? What do they want?"

"It's nothing to be frightened about, George. You are eligible for monthly benefits. You need to fill out an application. I will take you there if you want me to."

"Thank you, Dr. Philips."

While I was exercising, Mom talked with Angela about the upcoming concert. A new white shirt with a light-blue tie was lying

on my dresser, reminding me not to forget the event. Restlessly trying to shake the feeling of a change coming into my life tired me out.
I was fighting with myself ever since my mom put these pictures on
the wall that reminded me, at some time, I would meet the folks at
home. The truth is that I was in Germany and home in Oklahoma,
USA.

I asked myself, who does not want to go home? But I was afraid
to go home. I felt safe where I was and never thought that would
change until now. Talking with Angela did not help. She thought
meeting the new challenges would be wonderful. What can I do
about it?

Mother was counting the time until I would not need further
therapy and be released. It was springtime, and the letters from home
explaining all that needed to be done made Mother restless, and it
seemed there was nothing else to talk about but getting home. The
feeling of being abandoned was getting to me. Somehow, Mom did
not understand how fragile my hopes still were. Getting rid of the
hostility and anxiety that out of the blues just flared up.

I felt my hopes were crumbling by the hour. The fear of not
being able to keep up with my friends and family at home, mentally
and physical, enveloped me like a heavy, wet blanket. Mom spoke
of kids using computers in school. David, my eldest brother, had
bought more land and new farm machines that would help modern-
ize the business and bring success.

Where do I fit in? I wondered. *Do I really want to fit in?*

I was trying hard to build a belief system in which I would
become a normal person, with the constant help of therapists and
nurses pushing this wonderful future for me. The time would come
when I could forget about my artificial legs. The therapist worked me
hard twice a day, exercising quadriceps and hamstrings. Jim explained
reasons for rotating the inner thighs moving muscles in the buttocks
and knee joints.

I realized how fortunate I was that my amputation was below
the knees. I met guys who had to go through much harder tasks
because their amputations where above the knees, yet these guys were
the jokers and the kidders with staff and soldiers. We became a group

of hopefuls, and we learned from one another. Small talk and jokes kept us going.

Bob, a big man, spoke of being transferred to a rehab close to his parent's home after he was measured and prepared for his prosthesis. He mentioned that he was the only child and was adopted when both parents were fifty years old.

Shaking his head, he said, "I don't know how I will be any good to them when I get home." He continued telling us, the letters he received of the hope and wait for his homecoming would not be too long.

Stating that both, Mom and Dad where getting on in years. "What do I tell them?"

"My parents are the best any child could have." His voice faded.

I noticed tears in eyes of some, other buddies were cursing the war, and some were just shaking their heads. I want to be good to them, but there I was, stuck in that chair. Bill came up with a joke that he heard on TV to prevent Bob breaking into tears.

So it is—each of us carries a cross that we have to bear. It was that environment in which I felt safe, being with my buddies. But explaining that to my mother was not easy.

Talking about the future made me feel uneasy, and I had difficulties controlling my stumps as they jerked up and down. I am disabled and will be handicapped forever. But no one understood that when the talk about going home came up that the hopes that I accumulated was crumbling.

Each morning, I listen to the encouragements and picked up some new hope medicine as I called it. The loving care and patience around me gave me strength and courage. It was hard work to keep it together. How could I explain that battle to my family? Visualizing how I put one foot in front of the other, thinking of each step I was taking with these prostheses in fields on the farm? How could I be of help in any capacity on a farm? In time, I would become a burden to the family. Of course, they would not admit it, but let's face it—I am an invalid and family should understand my thinking. They should help me to become what I was best suited for, not that I knew what that might be.

Hours and days passed with unfriendly thoughts, and the wish of being with my buddy Joe somewhere in the clouds was on my mind a lot. I could not get out of my morose attitude. Jim waited for me each time with a pep talk, and Dr. Philip walked with me to stores and introduced me to men who were walking with their prosthesis.

CHAPTER 9

*L*ooking fabulous, Angela appeared in the room on concert night. She saw the tie and mentioned that it was the same colour as her dress.

"Sorry, I cannot go with you. I must be there early. Nevertheless, I ordered a taxi to take you. I will come home with you," she said.

"Are you nervous?" Mother asked.

She shook her head in response, blowing me a kiss, and out the door she was.

"How the hell? I can't remember how to tie this damn tie. Do I have to wear it, Mom?"

"You'd feel better when you see others wearing one."

Well, others don't come in a wheelchair either, I thought. Looking into her eyes, I knew all the effort was worth it.

"Mom, turn around for me please." Pride swelled in me. "You look beautiful, Mom," I said. "I am grateful you are here with me." By speaking these words, I realized that these were the first compliments I had spoken to my mother since she came to stay with me in this foreign land.

OK, everybody spoke English, and that made it easier for her; still, she was away from her farm, and I realized the sacrifice. Emotions overcame me, and I wanted to hug my mom; but this chair was in the way. She knew my needs and bent to hug me and held me for a while.

"I am so sorry," I whispered into her arms.

It was a handicap-accessible cab that picked us up. The driver spoke little English and pointed out the many cars parked already in the parking lot.

"Volles house" (Full house), he said.

A porter directed us to our seat. People were speaking German all around us. *Funny,* I thought, *I never heard the nurses speak in their native tongue.*

After a while, the lights flickered, and the room quieted. Someone spoke and introduced the orchestra, two choirs, and individual voices that made up the concert. It seemed that Angela was the only female soloist singing. I listened to the song from which I had run away at the chapel when she was practicing. Angela was introduced as a nursing student at the rehabilitation center in Land Stuhl and dedicated her song to the wounded soldiers. She looked tall and sat gracefully at the piano, playing the interlude and singing.

"*There is someone who loves every soldier. He is only a prayer away. This someone is called Jesus and heals every bone when we pray.*"

I was too embarrassed to wipe my tears, so I let them fall. I don't remember the rest of the lyrics, but each word seemed to speak powerfully to me.

The ovation was tremendous. At the end, Angela was given a beautiful bouquet of flowers. We traveled home in the same cab; apparently, it belongs to the center. I had never seen this building all lit up in the dark; it looked inviting and majestic.

"How welcoming it must be for my wounded comrades landing on peaceful ground and greeted by this staff," I said.

Folks were waiting for us. I heard greetings and congratulations spoken to Angela. The concert had been televised for the soldiers who could not attend. Only ten of us had actually been there. Dr. Kopp came to say hello and said, "Next time, you will walk into the concert hall."

We mingled around tables filled with appetizers. For a moment, I felt I belonged to the world, with hope for a future.

I noticed smiles on men who usually sit alone, not communicating much. Tonight, they were waving at me. In their eyes, I read sad and questionable stories. What were these eyes saying? What was their story, their grief, their mental anguish? We were all grieving, I knew, but what was the concentration of our eye contact? Some do not have family visits whereas I had my mother. Did these men miss their moms tonight? The tall man with the face of a boy who had spoken with my mom before seemed especially different tonight. I wondered whether he was lonely for his mother.

Well, George you feel different too. I wondered if I could do something for these individuals who mostly sat alone.

Not wanting to lose these thoughts and upbeat feelings, I said my good night early. I needed to be alone, reflect, and sort out my innermost soul. While my mother helped me to get out of these fancy clothes, I asked her if she believed those courageous words of Dr. Kopp that I'd be walking to the next concert.

Facing me, holding my face in her hands, she said, "Yes, son. I believe that with all my heart." She rubbed our noses together.

I fell asleep planning ways to help the men who had no visitors. These were profound thoughts giving me meaning for the next day. I would help these men in some way—be a comrade, a buddy.

As soon as I opened my eyes the next morning, the family pictures stared at me. The day started with that problem, and my previous night's thoughts vanished. I decided to talk with Mother and then maybe get Dr. Kopp involved. How? I could not go on with the secret of not wanting to go home. It was not that I did not love my family, but I could not see myself interrupting their life. I just did not feel right, and I could not tell Mother to remove the pictures either after all. So the day started with fighting myself, and it did not improve. Mom went shopping, and I spent most of the day alone. It was Saturday, so not much was going on.

A couple of weeks ago, I seemed to be on the road to mental recovery. I was interested in the environment; I watched the gardeners plant red, yellow, and blue pansies under trees and all around. Ever since I realized that the time would come when I needed to go home, my thoughts became worries. I rarely felt hate anymore, but it was difficult handling the uncertainty of what was to come, remembering Father Paul and Dr. Kopp's wisdom to pray when the light is dim.

"Great Spirit, enlighten me with ways and means to go on." I am so impatient and could not find any words, so I sat in the dark chapel alone with the eternal light. Somehow, it comforted me.

Lenten time was ending. Men were working, removing the purple cloth around the cross, replacing it with white cloth; and the bright-colored flowers and white lily plants placed around the chapel made the altar look so inviting. Easter Sunday is a very important holiday for Catholic people. I was brought up in that environment. I remember the emphasis on heaven and hell, how God punishes when we err from the straight and narrow.

Confession was the worst. Going in that dark booth and confess the candy bar I stole took courage. I cringed sitting alone in church, not daring to leave even one minute before the ten Our Fathers were said. It seemed so long ago. Was I preoccupied with my conscience, hiding my deepest thoughts from Mother that I want to stay here? These were similar feelings as in the confession booth.

Wait a minute, George, I thought. *I am a man now, grown-up, gone to war, lost good friends, and left my legs in the fields. God this is hell.* I needed to scream hell on earth. *How can I get this matter out of my mind and settled? I need to confess to Mom. There is no way around it.* I watched her move her fingers quickly with knitting some item. *Just like at home*, I thought.

"What are you thinking?" I said.

"Oh, I was thinking about home. You know, I left in such a rush when I heard you arrived in Land Stuhl. The kids told me they would handle the farm. You know, George, I have to give them credit. From what they write, they don't need me at all," she said. "Margaret wrote in the last letter that they were blessed with six new calves, and old Bessie gave them twins. George, you remember the old, red-and-white-colored Bessie, her udders hanging almost to the ground after she gave birth?"

Watching her talk was a joy; it was so easy to listen. I enjoyed these talks and imagining pictures of how it was at home but had no desire to be there.

"Mom, who pays for all this here? I mean, you being here for so long."

"I must say, George, that everything is so organized for the families of the wounded. Our government does all this. There is even a new housing project going on just outside the town for folks that want to stay. You know, full-sized apartments. They were talking of a kindergarten area for moms with children, being able to stay while their men recuperate.

"The people of this village are friendly, and it's almost like home. Most speak English—the ones I come into contact with, anyway. It is amazing. I live in a small apartment with a bedroom, living room, bathroom, and tiny kitchenette. I can make small meals, or I can go to the canteen that is open twelve hours daily. I see and talk with many wives and parents of men recuperating. As a matter of fact, I have made a few friends with whom I exchanged addresses.

"Yes, I was glad I came to be with you, son, during those very hard days and weeks. I believe you are on the mend and could be transferred home into a nearby rehabilitation center. That way, we can visit you while you're establishing yourself and get out of this chair."

Here is my chance, I thought. *I must tell her now.*

CHAPTER 10

*T*he knock on the door was Jim reminding me it was time to exercise. I was glad I did not have to face the hour of truth, yet it would have been the perfect opportunity.

I maybe talk with Jim, I thought, *but Jim does not like to converse when teaching. He wants me to think about counting and breathing. After thirty minutes with him, I am exhausted both physically and mentally. I am sure he knows it. Still, he has the nerve to tell me that in the morning we try for forty-five minutes.* He wanted progress, and I was grateful.

"OK, George. See you in the morning," Jim said.

On the way through the great hall, some fellows called me over for a chat. Someone was speaking of programs being offered to soldiers who were expected to stay for further assistance. Big Bob had difficulties and was allowed to stay, if he wished. In the meantime, he was allowed to take any of these educational programs to help him return to society when the time comes. Did I hear that right, only some folks can participate?

Dr. Kopp appeared, looked at me, and he said, "How about it, son?"

"I am interested," I whispered, afraid of hoping for too much.

"We will talk about it."

We were given a pamphlet and told to use the phone number on the bottom if we had questions. "Searching for classes we might be interested in. Let's see here. Language, computer, religious studies, and health care," Mike read to us.

"Religion classes that is absurd! Who the hell—and what kind of religion?"

Father Paul popped up and said, "It does not matter. Even if you are an atheist, you can learn from these classes. Matter of fact, universities like Harvard, Yale, and Princeton offer theology for business majors. For instance, you learn to engage in dialogue of diverse life commitments. Theology is a broad science. They equip students with leadership skills, flexibility, adaptability, and openness that are required in any business. Or you might like to teach the history of various religions. In that case, you need all the above."

"Here you are, son!" my mother said, patting everybody's shoulder, ending with a kiss for me. "I ran out of yarn and was thinking of going to my apartment."

"OK, Mom, I will walk you to the door."

There it was again—*walk*. Ever since Dr. Kopp mentioned that word, it jumped at me.

"It is almost dinnertime for you, George. Hope it is you favourite. See you in the morning. Goodnight, dear."

I rolled myself to the chapel to digest the news. I lit a candle to find inner peace. Here I was sitting in this chair disgusted, just twenty-two years old, without a formal education. *The promise of getting an education came after you served for a year. Instead, I come home a broken man. Where to begin? What is there for me? What do I want to do in my life to support myself and maybe a family?* I felt frustration and anxiety coming to the forefront, accompanied with fear. When will I be able to walk?

I looked at the ever-burning light in this otherwise dark chapel, and after a little while, I remembered my friend without hands and his beautiful daughter's words behind his chair, saying, "God needed daddy's hands for a while." How much patience, determination, and time did his family need? I prayed for their well-being.

Thinking of others relieved my anxiety as it did now asking the Almighty for guidance in choosing the profession that was right for me. I felt a new gift awakening. My faith in the spirit believing help will come by praying, telling my troubles, and the challenges of the men and women around me seemed to visit me oftener. The explosions of anger and the hate for the warmongers in the world did not control my whole being as it had before. I admitted that Mom's and probably other folks' prayers did not go unheard.

What a wonderful world it could be.

I heard the bell for dinner; it gave us fifteen minutes to prepare. I was hungry. These sounds reminded me of home Sunday mornings in Apache Village where we lived and farmed our land.

I was the last one at my table. The conversation was about the opportunities for our future.

"Well, George, what classes are you thinking about taking, being the youngest among us?" Bob the salesman at General Motors did not think he would ever go back to his job.

I listened to each one, and no one mentioned healthcare. Maybe they thought that nursing was a sissy profession and was meant for women. Luckily, I did not have to answer the question as it seemed forgotten. The conversation changed to new hopes and great ideas.

I watched nurses, therapists, everyone working in the health field closely during the next few days. I met Angela walking with a fast stride, excusing herself for not having time to talk.

"Test time, George."

I was nervous as I watched her running past. The more I retraced what I was doing with my buddies here—feeding, listening, washing, or even reading to some—I enjoyed it. I was using my hands, the tools with which God left me.

Each day, new wounded came in need of help. Meaning, there would always be work for me as a nurse. This profession appealed to me more and more as I watched the staff working. It must be satisfying to be needed, just like how I felt when I did something for the newcomers.

Will the income be enough to feed a family? was my next question and a very important one. I remembered the nurses in the chopper, how fast they analyzed the needs of the wounded during emergencies. Never heard abusive or intolerant language, just fast acting to get out of danger.

Gee, what a life. Of course, it would not be that kind of nursing. I will talk with Jim my trainer and maybe Dr. Kopp of what they thought about the idea of me becoming a nurse during my appointment in three days. It seemed a long time to wait, and I felt anxious to share this important idea of me becoming a nurse.

I spent time in the library. There was Molly up high on a ladder, sorting books. I was amazed at how nimble the old lady was. She turned when I said "Hello."

"Haven't seen you for some time, George," she said as she climbed down with ease. She straightened her back in front of me. "Oh my, boy, that arthritis is giving me problems today. I tell you every day getting out of bed is a blessing."

I looked at her large hands with popping veins, loose skin marked with many brown spots, wondering how old Ms. Molly really was. Actually, we did not see old people around here. Maybe that was the reason I loved this helpful and friendly soul.

"Been busy, George?" she asked.

"Yes, working hard on getting out of here."

"So what brings you to me?"

"I am looking for nursing books."

"Of course, we have a large health care section. Come, I will walk you there."

In no time, I was carrying several books in my lap. She walked with me to a table.

"Let's sit here. The fire will warm my bones," she said. "Would you join me with a cup of coffee, or would you prefer hot chocolate?"

"Chocolate sounds great, Molly. Thank you."

I watched her limping back with two mugs. Carefully, she sat down, giving a loud moan.

"It is the dampness, George, that creeps into my bones. Otherwise, I feel fit as a fiddle."

Even though I was anxious to getting home and checking these books out—enjoying my hot chocolate, watching Ms. Molly nodding her head, her body sinking deeper in the chair, her hand still on the coffee cup—I felt a warm feeling of admiration for this person. I waited for Molly to wake up.

"What are you doing here?" Bob shouted, coming toward the table, awakening Ms. Molly instantly.

"Sorry George, but those minute naps feel good," she said. "Did you find something you want to take to the room?"

I handed her three to sign out for me, taking the books from my lab and replacing the signed out ones.

"Come again?" she asked.

I thanked her once more for the time and left.

I quickly wheeled myself out of the library to my room, hoping not to meet Bob. I found a nice hiding place for these books, just to avoid being asked questions that I could not answer. Even Mom should not know my idea for the moment until I was sure I was making the right decision.

CHAPTER 11

*D*r. Kopp, as usual, was in a jovial mood; and Jim, my personal trainer, met me at 3:00 p.m. I had no idea what I was in for with the two of them at the same time. I felt like a tiger caught in a net.

"How is the preprosthetic training coming, Jim?"

"George is doing well. I think he could do better if he was less preoccupied with—I don't know what. Right, George?"

"So what is it, George? What is bothering you?"

Here is my chance, I thought, but I was fighting for the right beginning.

"By the way, I met with your mother," Dr. Kopp continued. "She showed me all the pictures on the wall. Are you exited to see everyone?"

I could not explain what was going through my brain at that moment; however, after what seemed a very long time, I said, "That is my problem. You see, I don't want to go home, I want to stay here. How can I tell my mom without breaking her heart after everything she has given up for me?"

Again, I felt out of control and helpless as I sat in my bloody wheelchair—unable to run, unable to fight, a prisoner of war on friendly grounds. Feeling the pressure of having four eyes looking down at me to go on, I said, wiping my tears, "How can I work on the farm in my condition? I know I would be a burden and cause uneasiness in the family because no one would know what to say. You know, I feel like a heel since I know I can go home and I haven't told my mom that I do not want to go because I don't want to hurt her feelings. She sacrificed being here away from her farm.

"Look," I tried to explain, "I think, if I go to school here, getting an education while learning to walk again, I will feel better facing my family."

I felt relieved and wondered what next. Looking at the two men in front of me, I noticed the exchange of eye contact between Dr. Kopp and Jim. "Why did you keep that wish from us for so long, George? Why do you think we gave you Dr. Phillips to work with?"

"Well, the offer to go to school is new," I said, and I have decided to become a nurse or maybe a doctor."

Dr. Kopp shouted, "I am delighted to hear that, George. Wonderful, wonderful! You see, George, this is why you have to communicate. Do you realize how valuable the psychologist is with whom you are working? She can help and prevent any worry that hinders your recovery.

"Let's get going, we are wasting time. Let's see your skin with his fingers as he pressed various areas saying it is all nice and smooth. The scar has healed nicely, and there are no wrinkles. I am feeling here for subcutaneous fatty tissue, but all is tight and smooth. Feel here, George"—he took my hand and slid it under the kneecap—"this is very important. I tell you those men that did the surgery did an excellent job in the field, with minimal time and probably few tools. You should not feel any pressure while wearing your prosthesis.

"How are you doing otherwise, George? Are you training your upper muscle enough? Practicing getting in and out of bed or on and off the toilet? Are you able to turn from side to side without difficulties? What about phantom pain?"

I looked at Jim for the answer. I just was trying to believe what I heard. Someone understood why I had a good reason not going home.

Jim answered some of the questions and gave a general OK report about my work on working independently. "He continued adding more work. Massaging the kneecaps during a shower."

"Great, great, and don't worry about not wanting to go home or starting school. I will have someone come see you in the next few days. But tell your mom of your decision, I bet she will understand and will be helpful. I am happy to get another staff member. Congratulations, George. That is a great decision."

I had no words for how I was feeling but wheeled the chair to my room, like a tiger freed from its cage. Mother was sitting in her usual chair by the window.

"My goodness, what is the excitement, son?"

"Mom, I've got to tell you what happened. I am ready to start training to walk. Best of all, Mom, I can go to school here to become a nurse and work here while I am training to walk."

My heart pounded, and I felt exuberant until I noticed that Mom sat very still, not joining in my elation.

"Mom, is that not wonderful?" I rolled close to her chair, my hands on her knees, shaking her a little.

Slowly, taking my head in her hands, looking into my eyes, she said, "You really want to stay here, George? You don't want to see your family?"

"Yes, I do, Mom. But I must become independent first. I love my family so much that I don't want to be a hindrance. Mom, please understand." Not wanting to look at her pained face, I put my head on her knees, praying and crying at the same time. Her warm hand stroking me felt good, and I appreciated that mom was with me.

"You see, Mom, I did this all to myself, thinking I could get an education by going into the army learning and making you proud of me. I remember how you cried and begged me not to sign up. I realize how right you were. So, here is another chance. I want to try again to make you proud of me. Let me try, Mom. Please give me your blessing."

Moments without reaction felt like hours until, quietly but firmly, she lifted my face out of her lap and said, "Son, of course you have my blessing. I understand how you feel, but do not feel you were wrong signing up. You are a typical American who wants to do what is right for this crazy world. Don't worry about your family. We will support you in all that you do. If you feel you need to come home for a spell, that would add to all our blessings."

She held me and said, "My son, you are very precious to me."

"Thank you, Mom."

I felt her salty tears and lips all over my face. *Life couldn't get any better right now.* I did not want this powerful sensation going through every nerve of my body to end, how easy it all was. Again, I recognized all that fighting with myself—how to discuss my feelings with my family, worrying that they might not understand my need of me being with my buddies.

CHAPTER 12

O h, I had new ideas, a new vision, of what I can become staying in Germany. With all the fear gone, I was ready to take on anything, just as I had done when I left home and went to war a few years ago. Maybe my previous undertaking was a learning curve for the future goal. Who knows what was planned for me? *George, did you say that, hmmm?*

During the next week, my mom was busy shopping for gifts for family members. She showed me things for the baby and an ornament for my little brother. Mom asked for my opinion, but I could only come up with "Nice, Mom," and a smile. I was too busy with my own thought, my trainer, and my psychologist.

"I see you are riding high, George," Dr. Philips said, explaining my endorphins were working overtime, explaining that many patients feel that way when they are finally ready for the real thing.

"Believe me, there will be days of cursing in the near future. Please call me when you feel down, tired, or have any negative emotions," she added. "I am here to see that you will remain confident and upbeat as you feel now. This is an important time of your life. The best of us have dark moments, but with our patients, we don't want them to linger.

"We want to be of help so they recover quickly after a bout of hell on earth. There will be days you will curse. Both of us will evaluate your daily progress with efficiency and reevaluate our program as well as the long-term and short-term goals. Trust us, George, and have faith that the outcome will be a new life for you."

I spent more time in the library reading the nursing books that were given to me by the librarian. I had difficulties deciding what to study first—bones, skin, brain, heart, lung, arteries, and veins. The pictures revealed intricate details and the precision of our body's work that happens without much acknowledgement of the human thought.

I wondered whether the nurses knew the individual parts of the body as I waded through the pages. Maybe specializing in certain areas as the options come up would be the way to go. I became more and more interested in becoming a nurse, even feeling emotional about it. I was excited by how much I would be able to do for people. I had to wait another month for school to begin. In the meantime, we started with preprosthesis training. I showed Jim what I could do. He did not seem impressed.

"Fine," he said, "let's start from the beginning."

But I wanted him to know what I could to. I showed him the exercises I did—getting in and out of bed, turning from side to side, lifting my limbs up and down, holding them in the air and counting.

"OK," he said, "we need stronger muscles. We began with five times and work our way up."

I put weights on the end of my limbs and lifted and held them up. Lifting my buttocks off the ground was not easy but necessary to strengthen the muscles. I never knew that my butt had so many muscles. They became important while learning how to walk. It was all amazing stuff to me.

During the second week, I felt the stress, and my enthusiasm waned. Going through all the stages of exercise in the morning and repeat them in the afternoon while being watched and checked was tiresome. Finally, the morning came when Jim wheeled my chair between the bar. We put a socket over each leg and slipped the prosthesis on. I was to put my hands on one side of the bar and lift myself up with my arms into a standing position. I found out quickly how much strength that took and was glad for Jim's help. Now I was hanging with my upper body over the one rail as I was letting myself stand on my feet. Jim guided me and wanted to know what I was feeling.

Carefully, I stepped down and shifted weight from one foot to the next. Bending my knee and moving the legs one after the other was a task. I did not let go of my upper body from hanging over the bar.

Jim smiled at me and said, "If you let go and stand up straight, I would take a picture."

"Jim, I need to sit down. I am tired," I said.

Dr. Philips and Dr. Kopp came in and congratulated me on my effort.

"What effort? I am so scared of falling."

"Look over there. That is Larry's third day," the doctor said.

"He has a good leg to help him," I replied.

"True," she said, "but his difficulty is above the knee amputation, which has different learning challenges."

He was walking between the bars without holding on most of the time.

"Give it a day or two," Larry shouted, "and be grateful."

I wanted to try again. After a glass of water and evaluation of my heart rate and blood pressure, I repeated my exercise and felt better about it. I actually stepped hard on my feet and made side steps to the right and then to the left. *I am going to walk. I know I will.*

Larry, waved to me across the room, saying, "We are going to walk."

I laughed and cried at the same time, thinking, *I have hands and I have legs too. How great is that?*

Jim gave me some help taking my contraption off.

"Why can I not keep my legs, Jim?" I asked.

"I am afraid you might try some things that we both might regret," he said. "See you in the morning."

*Rat*s, I thought, but then, *could I really try walking, even standing up, without Jim being there? Unlikely. But why not?* I reached for my legs.

Wheeling myself to the chapel, I felt hopeful and energized. "God, it feels very good. Give me whatever it takes to keep it up. I want to work. I want to be useful. Amen," I prayed.

Angela came in to practice the organ for Sunday.

"Hey there, George," she said after kissing me on the cheek. "I haven't seen you for a while."

"How are you, Angela?"

"Relieved now. My third semester was difficult, and I studied hard to keep my grades up. I feel good having that behind me. Students tell me the fourth semester is easier, which begins in the fall."

It would have been appropriate giving her a hug and kiss to congratulate her. How I wanted to do that right now, but the dumb chair was in my way.

"What's the matter?" she said. "You are looking at me funny. What are you thinking?"

I told her, "No problem."

She said, "I need a hug and a kiss." Bending on her knees in front of the chair, we held one another for a short time.

"Let's go for a walk after I practice my music, OK?"

Not waiting for an answer, she hopped to the organ. I sat there not wanting to let go of that electrical current I was feeling. How surprising life can be at times.

Yes, I wanted to go for a walk, I thought, rolling myself to my room to refresh my looks for our date. Couldn't resist humming the song "Got a Date with an Angel" as I walked back to the chapel to meet that angel.

Yes, I will be walking soon. I just can't wait. I can't wait until I am independent, have money, drive a car, and take my angel to movies and dinner. Drive a car? Wait a minute. Yes, I do have a license—an American one. I need to ask how that works. I anxiously waited for Angela

Finally, she hopped off the organ and came to meet me. "Let's go, then," she said.

CHAPTER 13

*T*he air was clear and fresh. It was so quiet; just a few folks sat on benches. We looked for the first stars as they appeared and had fun seeing who could count the most.

"I have two weeks' vacation," Angela mentioned.

"Do you have a summer job?"

"Yes, you know I work as an aide right here in the hospital. The practical stuff I learn from seasoned nurses who help me understand how involved nurses are with a patient."

Do I dare asking her if she gets paid? It is dark, and I could ask now without looking embarrassed, I thought.

"Is that paid for?" I asked.

"Yes, after I help Mom at home a little and my grandma who works in the library. She wants me to dust areas that she can't reach."

"That's your grandma? She is such a lovely person. She helped me find some nursing books the other day. You know, I made up my mind to stay here and get a nursing education," I said.

"Well, that is wonderful news, George. Not surprising that you have chosen this occupation. You have that special humaneness about you and can sense the needs of others."

"I have?"

"Yes, so different from when you woke up. George, you were a hostile, angry, and sometimes even uncontrollable and speaking of suicide in your dreams the first four to six weeks."

"I don't remember much about that. But I do remember that I hated to wake up. I felt my body would burst any moment. I saw the

Iraqi people walking around us, not knowing what they might do to us any moment, and I was unable to defend myself."

"You screamed a lot and fought with your upper body, waving your arms like a madman until exhaustion overcame you. Usually, you ended up soaking wet. Your mother rarely left your side."

"In my dreams, I was in Iraq most of he time watching women with children giving us dirty looks or children pointing a finger at us as though it might be a gun shooting the soldiers.

"Angela, I tell you, if I had a gun, I would have used it. I could have killed anybody in my way and almost everybody was in my way, and I don't believe I knew that I had left my legs there."

"Yes, George, you were a dangerous person when first awake." She sat on a bench looking at me, and then she put her hand on my arm. "Look at you now, George, you got through the storm. I know you will make a great nurse with all that experience behind you."

I felt her hand on my arm and wanted to cup my hand over hers. But I was afraid she would move away, and I did not want to let this heavenly moment go. We sat quietly.

My thoughts drifted to my station in Iraq, wondering what my comrades were doing while I sat here safe with a beautiful girl. *I paid a hefty price*, I thought. *Was it worth it George?* I shouted an immediate "Hell no!"

"What was that all about?" Angela asked.

"Just thinking. Angela, do you believe we should be fighting in Iraq?"

"I don't know, dear. I really don't know what is going on. We learned about American history in school, I remember. They fought wars, but we did not learn about Asian history. There have been wars since beginning of time, and it seems that the human race has not learned to find ways and means to live side by side in peace."

I noticed Angela's legs dangling and my stumps starting to act up uncontrollably.

My hands tried to hide this, but she was aware and asked, "Is that painful, George?"

"No, not really. Just thinking, will I be able to do such simple things with my new legs?"

"Sure, you have seen how scientific your prostheses are made. This time next year, we will sit here and you will have finished your first year in nursing and we will be both dangling our legs."

After a long while of quiet and many mixed-up desires, I said, "I hope so." I looked into her smiling blue eyes.

"Let's see. How long have you been here, George? We met around Easter time. You have been here about two months. You must have been very ill. The usual length of stay is forty-five days."

"I was told that I lost a great deal of blood and fought a blood infection. After I was in staple condition, they removed some shrapnel from my upper right and left arm. I feel good now, except being confined in this chair drives me crazy. I can't wait to walk. Still, when I think of having to strap those contraptions on my limbs, I get furious at times and think of all the wrongs humans are committing in the name of defending our country."

"Stop right there, George. These thoughts get you in trouble, and you know it. When you let yourself think of right and wrong in the world, your anger becomes uncontrollable and you lose your sense of now. You have a lot on your plate. Use your energy to walk and build a career for yourself, to be able to live a normal life with family and friends. That is your new goal and your duty to society. Be a guide to other people who are struggling."

"I guess you are right, Angela. I think that is part of the reason why I want to stay here and help the fellows that are coming in daily. You know, I think so often about the mates that I left out there and I am afraid for them."

"Best remedy is prayer, George. Tell me, why do you want to stay in Germany to go to school? Not that I don't like the idea, but you can go to school at home too. Wouldn't the language be a problem?"

"I thought about that, but the books are all in English. I don't know if it will make sense to you, Angela. I feel so close to my mates that I left out there struggling in combat without sleep, and when there is the odd time, you cannot fall asleep due to fear or even homesickness."

"So much goes on in your brain," Angela said.

"I also believe I can help the fellows that are still coming in daily."

"I agree, and it is a good psychological stimulant for yourself." She smiled.

"How come you know so much?" I said, looking into her eyes which matched the colour of her sweater.

"Gosh, George, you have given me so much news, I am having trouble taking it all in. What about your mom? She is leaving tomorrow evening and arriving in Oklahoma City late afternoon."

"Yes, she has chosen the night flight so that she will not waste time looking around at what all has happened while she was away. I must see her to say goodbye. Maybe we could have something to eat together at lunch. Surely the boys want to see her too."

"Leave it to me. I will arrange something."

The noise of an airplane made us look up and behold uncountable stars looked down on us. *Very nice.*

"I remember a song about catching a star," Angela said.

"I do too. My mom taught it to us while walking uphill tobogganing."

"Let's go in, George, it is getting chilly. What are you going to do now, George?"

"I'll watch TV for a while."

"OK, then I'll go home. Good night, dear, until tomorrow."

CHAPTER 14

S ure enough, the next day, a large table was set with flowers, plates of sandwiches, and soft drinks. Dr. Kopp, my therapists, and all were invited to wish Mom a good trip home. Angela brought her grandma and introduced her to Mom. We listened to good words and friendly suggestions from all. Grandma Molly hugged Mom and told her not to worry, reassuring her that they would take care of her boy. Both of them looked at me.

Suddenly, the truth hit me—my mom was really leaving Germany and I would be alone, fending for myself very soon. I watched her patting some men on the arm and some on the head, kind words sounded through the dinning room, and it was downright spiritual; or maybe having my mother around raised my spirits. We walked slowly back to our room after the staff thanked my mom for her help during those difficult times. Mom sat in her usual chair, empty-handed. Her knitting things had been packed. I moved close enough to be able to take her hands and kissed them. Our teary eyes told the story. No words were necessary.

After a while, she lifted my face, kissed it, and said, "I have one more goodbye to say, dear, and then I have to get ready for the airport. A taxi will take me. I will call you as soon as I get home. I love you, my hero, George."

With that, she walked out of the room. She looked so straight and tall. I sat in my chair, spellbound, and then I saw Angela standing in the door.

"I thought you might like some company, George. I brought some papers from my first semester of nursing. We could go through them, if you wish."

Although I felt exhausted, I did not want to be alone, and I thanked her for coming.

"Wow! There are a lot of papers."

"Well, this is the way I practiced. Writing things down helps me remember. You might not need to do that. We can dispose of some when you are through with them. But my tests are there, and they might be of use to you. I don't imagine they would change too much from year to year, though they might be differently worded."

"Look at all the As.

"I need to have a 3.0 grade point average to receive my financial help."

"Maybe I can apply for that too."

"Why not? You should give it a try, George."

"Angela, before anything, I need to walk. I am so frustrated it takes so long to become independent. I am told that I am making normal progress, but I tire so fast."

"What do you mean, dear? You are independent now. You are making decisions. It is not only your exercising that tires you. It's all the change that happened at once. You need to be patient because your impatience is robbing you of more energy."

"Angela, you are so smart."

"No, George. It is not that at all. I just see things from a different perspective. You see I can speak with ease, but I never went through hell like you did. I want to see what you are doing. Can I come when you are exercising?"

"I don't know, Angela. I'm not sure whether I want you to see me holding on to the bars for dear life."

"Don't be silly," she said, patting my head.

"OK, three thirty."

"I will see you there. I imagine you could do with some rest now." She waved her hands and left.

Damn it, everything seems so easy when listening to that woman. Again, she runs before I can respond. I don't know, maybe it is too early to let her see me struggle. I will ask the therapist to tell her so when she comes this after noon. Angela, Angela, I don't want to lose your friendship, but every time you talk to me, I feel so inadequate, downright helpless. You behave like a big sister, and I don't want that. Hell, I don't know what I want. I must have dozed off. When I woke up, I rushed to therapy.

CHAPTER 15

I drove right to the bar.

"Wait a minute, you forgot your legs," Jim shouted, sitting on the bench beside my prosthetic legs.

Damn it, first mistake, I thought. I was in a hurry and did not want Angela to see me putting them on.

"You are anxious. "What seems to be the matter?"

"Nothing, nothing! This girl, Angela, wants to watch me exercise. Could you tell her to come back in a few days? Jim, please, I don't feel like I am ready."

After getting my socks over my limbs and the prostheses, making sure there were no wrinkles anywhere, I wheeled myself to the bar. Jim stood beside me watching, not saying a word, while I grabbed the bar and pulled myself out of the chair to stand on my legs.

"Great!" Angela shouted from the doorway. "Jim, can I come in and watch?"

Looking at me for approval, he said, "Come on in."

I took some test steps, two to the right and then moved left.

"Try both bars, George, I am behind you. Just turn a little. Trust your legs. They will hold you."

I pivoted the right leg to the right and grabbed the other bar.

"It's OK, your legs will hold you. Don't lift yourself up so much. You're using your arms too much. Push your body into the legs and walk. Here, I put the chair in between the bars so you can sit down when you need to."

"No, no, put it at the end of the bar in front of me so that I can look at this wheelchair for the last time," I said.

"I believe you are rushing it a little, George," Jim said.

I walked to the end, and Angela received me with open arms, shouting, "You did it. Let's do it again."

I didn't know whether to laugh or to cry. Seeing myself in a mirror not too far from me, I said, "There I am a grown man, with all my extremities." *So tall—yes, that is me.*

I raised myself up, using the same procedure as before.

Yes, I thought, *I can trust these legs, and I am in control of my legs.*

At the other end, Angela was waiting, but my arms gave up and I needed to sit down in the middle.

Jim walked over to Angela and gave her a hug. "How have you been? Long time no see."

"Just one more semester," I heard her say as she danced a little jig toward me. "Hello, my hero," she said and hugged me too.

"What is this, the hugging committee?"

"We hug a lot around here," Jim said. "We are a big family and support one another any time of day, needed or not, right, Angela? So, tell me, Angela, what have you been doing? I have not seen for some time."

"Been busy with school. Today, I am going to see some friends. If George feels like it, I'll take him for a walk."

Angela handed each of us a small cup of milkshake. Jim and Angela were sitting on the floor. I was in my chair. While the two were engaged in conversation, I was spinning ideas of possibilities in my new life. I was trying to remember a poem; I forgot who the author was. It read, "Why reach for the lowest star, when you can reach for the highest?"

With a new life, a door's wide open for me to look in to and explore. Best of all, I am equipped with the tools I need—my mind, my physical body intact, and my returning faith.

"OK, Jim, awaken me out of spinning dreams," I said.

"Let's do some more work, George."

Angela waved as she left.

Then I lifted myself to walk. The optimism I felt gave me energy. Each step forward felt like I was walking on fire as I made my way between those two wooden sticks.

"I need pants to cover this metal, Jim. I don't want anybody to know that these are not my legs."

"There is a store downstairs where you can get all you need. By the way, have you applied for your VA benefits as yet? You should probably do that soon. Your counsellor will help you with that, George. Don't worry. The Department of Veterans' Affairs should have been knocking on your door by now."

"Not so," Dr. Phillips quipped, having overheard the conversation as she waltzed into the room. "You have to go to them. They have changed the rules. I will go with you in the morning, George. I see you making great progress with walking."

"Show Dr. Phillips."

"OK, thank you for coming with me." Again, I walked through the bars.

"Show-off." Jim smiled.

Everybody seemed satisfied with my progress, except me, I thought while taking off my contraptions.

Not long after my exercises, Angela showed up. I asked if she would go to the store with me rather than going for a walk.

"OK, good idea. Maybe you want to eat dinner at McDonald's? It's right beside the store."

"Great. Wait, Angela, I don't have any money."

"That's OK. You can pay me back when you have some."

We took the elevator down, and there was a whole new world that opened up to me.

"Angela, this is just like an army surplus shop. I have not been anywhere for so long. I could go nuts in here. I need so many things. I am looking for a pair of pants to cover my legs."

"Look at this crazy shirt. Do you like these colors, George?"

"I love red—all kinds of red. I think that color looks good with your blonde hair."

"OK, what size?" she asked.

"Heck, I don't know. The last pair of pants had a number of thirty-eight, and that fitted me. I don't want to be seen in red pants."

"What about this beige colour and a red shirt?"

"Yes, I think I like that. Will you come shopping with me when I have money?"

"I'd love to, George."

"Let me see." Angela took the measuring tape from the clerk and measured my waist.

"I wish I had waist size thirty-eight."

After a long time touching and inspecting all kinds of electronics, we walked to McDonald's and ordered a Big Mac each. Neither had much to say, just enjoying each other company and the food. It had been a great day, thinking of all the things that happened. I fell asleep with a grateful feeling in my heart.

Dr. Phillips appeared promptly the next morning at the breakfast table, ready to assist me with the Department of Veterans' Affairs. It was in the same vicinity where Angela and I were yesterday.

"You should not have a problem, George, receiving a nice pension."

"I hope."

"Have you decided where you want to live after you are discharged from here?"

"Could I not stay in my room and pay rent until I am able to walk without help?"

"I am not certain, but we could ask as Dr. Kopp might have some influence in that department. Why would you want to live in a hospital environment, George?"

"I feel comfortable here. It's been my home for some time. Yes, I feel grateful to all who helped me staying alive."

I was asked many questions by the clerk, some that I could not answer but could be found in the file that came to Germany from the field. After signing many papers, we were told that I should have my first paycheck within a month.

"I have to wait that long?"

"You can get credit to help you, Mr. Reynolds. The bank is in the same building."

Dr. Philips walked with me, and in no time, I counted one hundred dollars in my hand but no wallet.

"Let's wait and see what is in your file, George. You probably had a wallet and it ended up in a paper bag."

"Private George Gregory Reynolds, is that you?"

"Yes, ma'am that's me."

"Can you prove it?"

"Wait a minute. No, I can't."

"What about your tag around your neck?"

"Oh yes, I forgot about that."

The army tag in the wallet had the same number as the tag around my neck.

"Yes, that is my stuff," I confirmed as the clerk emptied the envelope on the counter. The picture of my mom was the first thing I saw falling on the counter. It was dirty from taking it out to look at in the field. Seeing her smiling eyes when I felt afraid had been a blessing to me. I held it for a minute, kissed it, and put it with my belongings.

"Have a good day, Private Reynolds. Thank you, Miss."

Dr. Phillips pressed her hands on my shoulders, walking quietly beside me. After controlling my emotions, I invited Dr. Philips to a hamburger.

"George, you have an appointment with Jim, remember. Another time. I will gladly take you up on that offer."

"OK, I am not going to forget it. Thanks for spending time with me."

I held my precious envelope, which contained everything I owned, close to me. There was not enough time to go through it now, but after my walk with Jim I will inspect it all.

"You are doing great this morning, George," Jim said.

"I feel great, Jim. I don't know how to explain it—it's like a heavy sack of bricks fell off me now that I have my stuff back, combined with the knowledge that I am really going to walk. Dr. Phillips helped me get my pension, and we got my stuff back. The funny thing is, I never missed it, but it sure feels good to have it all together again. Would you call that an independent feeling?"

"Yeah, I guess so. Great, George, have some rest, and I will see you this afternoon."

I raced to my room to look at what was mine. There she was—my mom smiling at me as I opened the wallet. On the other side was a picture of the family behind my horse Ella, who knew all my secrets. *A little cross between more pictures and, for heaven's sake, who is that, Amy? How the heck did you get in my wallet?*

Amy, the little girl with so many freckles and long braids, we started school together. It ended when her mother could not afford payments for Catholic school. Not living far from us, she rode her horse to our house frequently, remembering she wanted to be my big sister, telling me how and what to do. I sat there trying to picture what she might look like now. She is as old as I am, maybe even married. "Oh well."

I found some Iraqi dinar (money) and two twenty-dollar bills. The smaller envelope contained some formal papers of my deployment and a rosary that my mom gave to me. That was it. I put the borrowed money into my wallet and the wallet in my shorts. I felt an uplifting energy; it was less intense but just freer. I could not explain it. I liked myself and thought of how changes in life can happen so quickly, one way or another—how fast I lost my legs and how long it took to feel myself again.

Actually, things are the same, I thought. My first goal in life ended up in failure. My legs will be artificial forever, but still they help me to walk again; therefore, not all was lost. I remembered the girl in the doorway, telling me that she will come back with her daddy to get some hands. I looked at my hands, thinking of all the things I can do with them daily. How very lucky I am to have met her. She was the first person to pull me back, to realize how much worse life can be without hands

How he is doing? I wondered. *Would he return to Germany?* And then I wondered about buddy who died so quick and young, unable to see and love his baby. *Joe, Joe, I miss you right now.* I thought of my mom's words when I was lying in bed not wanting to see anybody, "Have faith, son."

Where does all that faith come from in these individuals? I knew Mother prayed a lot on the farm. Rain or shine, Sunday mornings were special. It started with the smell of onions and fried potatoes coming from the kitchen, and I remember her voice sterner than the previous voice. Church was important to Mom, and just as important was not to disturb people; therefore, we should not be late. But I cannot imagine that Mother's faith came from only going to church. Come to think of it, Mother prayed all day. She did not seem hurried and always smiling.

It was a simple life on the farm. Everybody knew their chores; and if we messed up, we paid the consequence. I had come a long way. Filled with great emotion and gratefulness, I thanked God for those blessings. After lunch, I rolled myself to the chapel and just sat there. I had no words, but I knew the Spirit would let me know when to talk; and after a while, I spoke the names of the fellows I left in harm's way. I asked for God to please keep them all safe. I felt as though I was speaking with an old friend. It was good to talk of the needs I had.

Besides my therapy sessions, I visited the library and ventured outside the park. I had not heard or seen Dr. Kopp for some time and wondered if he was done with me. New questions kept creeping up. I had slacks now, but I needed shoes too. This challenge was brought up at the next meeting with the prosthetic.

Ms. Hilde appeared to be middle-aged woman. She looked at me through thick glasses. Her light brown hair in a bun made her appearance look stern, but her smile was warm and friendly. She watched me putting my prosthesis on and walk with them on the bar.

"How do they feel, George, do they press anywhere?"

I said, "No, they feel OK."

"Do you have any question, George?"

"Yes, I need shoes."

"One thing, George, never buy cheap shoes for yourself. They need to be fitted and evaluated. Otherwise, you will harm your body—back pain, blisters, imbalance while walking, and the end result is falling. Take heed and let us help you when you are ready to shop for shoes. You know, these shoes are expensive, but with regular maintenance, shoes last a long time. Consider what color you want them to be. They should have the color that go with your wardrobe."

"Do I take them off every night like normal?" I asked.

"That is up to you, George."

"How much longer before I can wear before I can wear my legs all day?"

"Give it time."

"How long?" I asked.

"You tell us, George. What do you feel when you walk the bar? Are you ready to try the crutches or maybe walk behind your chair? There is no rushing. You need to feel secure and ready. We understand your anxiety. Jim is your leader. Do as he tells you."

"Well, I thought by the time I go to school, I would be ready to walk without help. We will see."

I was glad when Ms. Hilde was done with the inspection. She handed me a card and wished me good luck. Jim asked me if I was OK doing some walking.

Grandma Molly greeted me at the library with a friendly smile. "Hello, son. Angela just left, she was here all afternoon dusting those upper shelves for me. What is this with your sad face, honey?"

"Nothing really, nothing goes fast enough for me. I think that is all, Ms. Molly. I wonder how long I will be sitting in this chair?"

"Angela tells me you are walking the bar."

"True, but I am still wheeling myself when getting from here to there."

"Give it time, George. Remember where you were a few months ago. It is known that during the transition time, folks lose enthusiasm and their willingness to go on. Often those men end up in the chair for the rest of their lives. You are not one of them. You have a goal and a strong determination. The world needs folks like you.

"I believe that any person with a willingness to persevere can go anywhere and get anything with prayer. Praying keeps your hope alive. I am sure your mom taught you that. Let's have a cookie. Angela baked them for me this morning. I will get some coffee. Will you join me?"

"Mmm, these cookies smell like Christmas.

"They are good. It's the cinnamon you smell."

"Reminds me of home, Ms. Molly."

"Tell me, have you been around our village yet, George?"

"How would I get around not walking?"

"You will, you will. She mentioned that the buses here are wheelchair friendly. The village is small but very up to date with accommodating soldiers. Tell you what, I'll pick you up for Sunday mass at St. Jude's. You will meet the rest of the family. I think that's a great idea. What do you say, George?"

"Great! I don't do anything on Sundays. It is very quiet here."

"Have you met Angela's mother yet? She is my daughter, you know. And a hardworking woman. She buys all that stuff that you see in the surplus shop. She orders it, inspects the merchandise, and makes the decision whether it is usable and practical to sell."

"She must be smart."

"Yes, I think she is very sensible. She talked to the folks around here to find out what they want to see in the store. Not long ago, a bunch of computers came in from China. She and some other office worker used them, decided that they were second hand. In spite of a good deal, they sent them back. She takes the negative comments are necessary to listen to. I have three girls and two boys. Don't want to brag," she continued. "I think they all turned out to be good human beings."

"How else could they have turned out with a mom like you, Ms. Molly?"

"Must say, it was not always easy."

"By the way, you speak English like I do. Does everybody in this town speak English?"

"You'd be surprised. Most everyone speaks some because of the hospital when the Americans built this hospital to prepare it to be the medical center of Europe for the severely wounded coming from Iraq and Afghanistan. Most all other regional centers closed up like Frankfurt, Berlin, Munchen, and others because the airspace close by was safe and fast to get the wounded treated. Americans spent millions and still building. It is known to be the very best in Europe.

"Right now, they are building more modern units for families that want to be close to loved ones. It's amazing. You can see why it is beneficial that we speak English. It seems to be the universal language. People come from all over the world. Tourism is big business here in the summertime. The town became worldly. Hotels and restaurants shot out of the ground. This quiet village has grown in tourism and elegant shops ever since. You see the airbase is not far from us here, you will see. Maybe you will make this your own town and have your family visit you."

"You are getting me all excited, Ms. Molly. Thank you for the coffee and cookies."

"It is Wednesday, four more days until Sunday. Maybe by that time, I will walk a little behind the wheelchair."

On the way to therapy, I noticed John walking with just a cane. "You look great, John. How are you doing? I haven't seen you exercising lately."

"Hi, kid. What do you think I am doing? Walking is exercising. I can hardly believe it. Not long ago, you barely walked with the crutches. That was hard, not that this is much easier. I am always afraid I'll fall and do harm, but I am told that uncertain feeling will go away in time."

"Anyway, you look great. No one would think you had an artificial leg."

"Don't be fooled, George, you know when you have one. Believe me. It will be your life's companion."

I noticed how carefully he was sitting on the bench. "Are you having pain?"

"Off and on. It is the phantom pain that bothers me more."

"That is funny, John. Phantom pain is when your legs move up and down because mine do too, especially when I am excited. My pain is in my own leg. Sorry to hear that. I like your shoes, John. Where did you go for them?"

"I like them too. I had them specially built for me, just down by McDonalds. You will be able to get a pair made when you have to match one that gets expensive. Make sure you have help in fitting them."

"I am told that I have time for that."

"You can do that anytime. Why wait? Shop a little. It passes the time and might get you acquainted with normal living."

"Have you been in town, John?"

"I took a cab twice this week. Interesting place, so clean and the people are friendly. Everybody speaks English. You can pay with euro or American money. Good restaurants, lots of music, and beer *Stuben* [a beer bar] on every corner. No dumps anywhere. I am flying home in two weeks, but I might come back here with my wife to live. She has to see how beautiful things are here. We have three kids, and it is not easy for her to think of uprooting my family."

"That is quite the undertaking you're asking of her."

"You are right, but once she comes for a few weeks, she will like it. I am a bookkeeper and believe that I can find work here. The children would be bilingual. Those are my goals."

"Goals, goals. I had a goal not so long ago. Look what happened to me."

"The ups and downs of life, my friend. You are young and will make more goals and break some more before you have gray hair. Don't ever get discouraged, George, keep on planning. It is healthy, and it gets you somewhere. Keep your mind and body healthy. Nobody owes you a living. You are responsible for yourself, and if you keep that up, you can be responsible for others.

"Trust yourself to know what you need. Find people you like and trust them to help you heal. Never ever accept that any condition is beyond help. One more thing, don't do drugs ever or alcohol. A beer here and there is fun. Always know your limits, George. What the hell, that's enough preaching for one session. So long, son. See you."

Watching him slowly getting out of his position and standing for a minute as if he had to get stabilized on his feet was enough to make me cry. Yet this is a man with a new goal, and what an undertaking it was—three children immigrating to a strange country. "What a man. He certainly could give good advice sounding just like Father Paul."

"You are late, George. Yes, sir. I am sorry, Jim." While I was putting on my socks, I told him that I met John. "Was John your client, Jim?"

"A couple of times when his therapist was sick."

"You know he wants to move his family here from the USA to this town. Imagine that."

"Nothing new. You read the newspaper, it tells you of how many folks come here from all over the world wanting to live here. George, lets get going."

I noticed Jim watching me carefully. I felt good about my independence.

"You are doing great, George. Do you want to try something else?"

"How did you know, Jim? I was thinking of trying to walk behind my wheelchair."

"That might work with someone sitting in it. Otherwise, you will tip over."

"I was thinking of learning with crutches. But let's see what I mean by you going behind the wheelchair."

"Come here, Frank, sit in this chair."

Looking perplexed but obeying the call, Frank sat in the chair. Jim was behind me as I was trying to get up from a bench holding on to the wheelchair.

"First mistake, George. You need to make sure that the brakes are locked so that it cannot move on you."

"It was hard standing up."

"What do you feel, George? Why was that so difficult?"

"The handle is much lower than the bar."

"Do you realize how much weight you put on these handles? If it was not for a heavy person sitting in it, you would have a danger-ous accident by tipping it over. Frank, take the brake off and brake with your feet when George feels like running. Straight, George, stand straighter, bend your knees, press into your legs, and go. You're OK, do it for a spell."

I am walking, John. I wish you could see me, Big John. Mom, I am walking out of the chair. Four more days until Sunday. I am going to do it. Thoughts were running away with me.

"Thanks, Jim, for everything. Thanks, Frank, for your help."

"Anytime, buddy."

The excitement of having been able to do what I just dreamed about a few hours ago was confirmation of what Ms. Molly had said in the morning. I felt powerful, at the point of no return.

"Jim, I was hoping that I would be walking into the church on Sunday."

"Don't push, George. This is dangerous thinking of you. Yes, I do understand how and what you feel. But please, please don't be careless. Falling at this stage of your progress would probably send you back to the beginning."

"I understand, Jim. I promise not do anything foolish."

The chapel was the place where my heart would stop pounding and my mind could get a hold of itself.

Days became nights, and nights turned into days again.

I made daily progress, spiritually and physically, until I heard the sirens on Saturday afternoon. Flashing lights and the sound of helicopters brought not only dust but that heavy feeling of what might be coming in. Nurses and physicians were informed of a stable and a fatally wounded individual. Watching people in green and white uniforms rushing around, I noticed lights being turned on two surgical suites.

"George, stay out of the way."

I huddled in my chair, not far from the entrance for a long time. I was located far from the wounded. I did not want to be alone and ended up in the TV room.

Too noisy there, I thought and fled to my room. I imagined where those guys came from, what happened, or if ever they were dads, sons, or brothers of someone. I wondered about my buddies, how they were doing at this moment.

This is not a good night. Too quiet there. I drove through halls and found no one around. *Where the hell is everybody?*

Frank's door was open.

"Come in, George. I was hoping for some company. I guess you feel the same when you hear a copter and sirens, your nerves seem to jump and lose control."

I looked at him and thought he was pale and old looking. "Will I ever understand the necessity of war? I am just as patriotic as the next American guy, but tell me, Frank, please make me understand. Why are we fighting six thousand miles from home, a society that has been fighting hundreds of years amongst themselves? What do we want from them?

"Don't look at me as if I was insane, Hank, just help me because when I think of how we are fighting in that heat, strapped with our armor for safety, yet the fear is always with us, facing the townspeople not knowing if he or she will pull a gun on me, was harder than being on the front fighting. What about you, Hank? Were you afraid?"

After pouring himself a drink and lighting a cigarette, he said, "Kid, you are talking above your head. Where is your patriotism?"

"Hank! Don't call me *kid*. Patriotism, my foot. I left my legs there in the sand. What the hell did you leave there? Did you ever run for your life? Did you ever let go of your friend's hand, knowing he will never hold it again? Hell, I don't see anything wrong with you. Tell me, am I that ignorant? Tell me a good reason for being there."

"I did not say you are ignorant, George."

"You have that damn attitude about yourself, Mr. Know-It-All. Just look at me, Frank. For the rest of my life, I will go to bed without my legs, remembering that I am a cripple."

"I realize that, George, you did it for your country. Many of your comrades have given their limbs and have returned for active duty. I just recruited three more men from here."

"Did you say you are recruiting?"

After a long pause, reliving the scene at home at the kitchen table, sitting across from the recruiter telling me all the great things I would learn by signing up, nothing was being said about being shipped to fight a war. Yes, you will learn how to defend your country, if necessary. That was OK with me. I remember my mother standing behind me saying, "Think about it, son. Give it a week or two."

But I persisted and reminded Mom that when I finished high school, I could choose what I wanted to do and that was what I wanted. I signed up the same day.

Months later, my life was crushed, devastated, and I am broken-hearted, for what? What am I defending? I was letting my emotions run away with me, I needed to get away from this man. Looking at

79

him, I mustered the will to say, "Yes, you look like a Geronimo. Go for broke, thinking guy."

I left as fast as I could and returned to my room. Tears ran down my face. *What to do tonight?* I needed Mom. I tried to sit in the chair where she knitted, but it was too high for me to get up. So I put my head on the seat, resting in my armpits, and cried some more. I woke up feeling cold and called for a nurse to help me to bed.

RN Nancy wanted to know my problem. I asked about the soldiers who were flown in. She shrugged her shoulders. "Sorry, I don't know, but it is a very restless night, and staff are needed downstairs."

"Thanks for coming, Nancy."

"You look like you could use a sleeper tonight, George?"

"Yes, I do. Great, I'll take one. The bed was a good hiding place tonight. I hoped that the drug might help me get a good sleep."

"Sorry, I have no time to chat. Good night, George."

I heard Angela knocking, and she was amazed to see me in bed at nine in the morning.

"What is the matter? Did you forget about our date at Grandma's house?"

Drowsily, I remembered the night before with Hank. "Angela, I don't think I can go today. I really don't feel good."

"That is OK. Grandma is waiting in the car. I'll tell her, but I am coming back. I want to hear what kind of troubles you accumulated last night."

She returned in no time with coffee and muffins.

"I can't eat, thanks."

"Well, I'll eat both of them," she said, making a face at me.

Seeing her enjoying food, I sat up and joined her without talking. Watching the sun making circles on the wall mellowed my anxious mind. Slowly, I got out of my misery.

Before starting to eat my muffin, she put it in my face and said, "Are you sure you don't want it?"

I shook my head and thanked her.

"George, it is so beautiful outside. Let's go for a ride. It will do you good to get out of your room. I will just say good morning to

Nancy. She was here all night. It must have been very busy. I'll be back in about thirty minutes to give you time to be ready, OK?"

So, I got ready for Angela, realizing that it would not be good to brood in my room, and that is what I should be doing. The valium from last night left me feeling kind of drowsy this morning.

"Ready, George? Let's get out of here. Nancy is dead tired, and I am quickly driving her home and Grandma to church. You come with me. Nancy will help me get you in the car. You will sit in the front so you can enjoy the scenery. Watch, you'll fall in love with our town."

After leaving Nancy at her house, we drove Ms. Molly to the church.

"Off we go into the sunshine," said Angela. I heard church bells and pictured going with my family up the dirt road to church, when Angela said, "Are you sure you don't want to go in? Grandma is disappointed. You know that, don't you?"

"Let's surprise her then," I said.

I wondered why Ms. Molly had not spoken with me in the car. Angela had to park on the road and brought the wheelchair to the sidewalk. I had to lift myself up out of the car, and Angela lifted my legs out in the wheelchair.

I cursed all the way, feeling embarrassed about being driven across the street into the church. I noticed three wheelchairs standing in the hallway and wondered to whom they might belong. I swore that mine was not going to sit there the next time I came to church. The music was playing as we walked in. Angela drove straight to the pew that belonged to the family Harris.

I slipped out of my chair and onto the bench beside Ms. Molly who gave me a big hug, whispering, "I prayed you might come."

A call to rise and the number of the song to sing was given. Folks reached for their songbooks, and I heard some throats clearing. The priest walked with two altar boys to the altar, and the mass began just like home, or so I thought.

When the messages were read, I remembered as a little boy, we had to think of what we might confess before going to communion. "Did I have anything to confess?" I asked myself.

The talk with Hank came to mind, asking, Am I really unpatriotic to my country? I suppressed the thought because Hank was a recruiter and probably never was at arms, and I did not want to feel angry. This was church, and I was sitting safe between two peaceful friends.

I wondered how old the church was. I marvelled at the artwork of rich dark oak around. The benches were recovered lately with a reddish tone of thick satin material. The stained-glass windows brilliantly displayed biblical stories by the morning sun. To the left was a small altar of Mary holding her baby. Above the main altar, there was a painting of the last supper—Jesus with his twelve disciples. I folded my hands and sat as the folks got up and down as the mass progressed, like it was done in Catholic churches. Ms. Molly asked if I wanted to go to the communion table, but I declined, causing too much commotion.

I told her, "Next time, I will walk with you," and our eyes met, smiling.

She patted my hand and said, "I know, I know, son."

Everyone stood before the Gospel was spoken. The organ music, together with the choir singing the "Alleluia," sounded beautiful; and the powerful voice of the priest speaking the Gospel gave me chills.

The lines to communion seemed unending. I knew the melody of the song being played, and then the words came to me and I sang, "This day God gives me strength of high heaven." There are no words to describe my feelings, and I did not notice that I sang in English as smiling faces passed me and crossed over me to get into their seats. That is how it used to be. *Gosh, Mom. Yes, Mom, I hear you.*

"George, you should sing in the choir." That seemed so very long ago.

After the bustle of communion, I heard the priest mention a baptism of a baby. I sat between my two ladies, and we stayed for the ceremony. I watched someone picking up a little girl to light a candle and noticed her eyes in the light. I remember my mom picking up my little brother to do the same and wondered if my eyes would look like his in the light. Always, Mom would ask on the way home, "For whom did you light the candle, Peter?"

And he would kick stones and say, "I don't know."

Then my mom would say, "We light a candle for the soldiers far from home that they might come home soon."

I needed to light a candle after the baptism and asked Ms. Molly to help me.

Angela popped up and said, "I'll do it for you."

"No, no. That's not the same. I need to do it." This light had to go straight to heaven for the comrades that I left fighting without me. I pictured each one of them in my mind. I did not want to blow out the match thinking I might blow out their life. "Holy Mary, please, please pray to your son for these men, my buddies."

"Grandma, I want to show George the town for a little bit. Is that OK?"

"You do that. I will get lunch ready."

We drove to the farm and left Ms. Molly at the gate. I did not want to talk and was happy Angela seemed to understand. She pointed to some buildings and mentioned that American architects had built them and moved here. We drove around the airbase but could only see how large it was. After an hour, I felt so tired, and Angela suggested to put the seat down so I could rest before meeting the family.

I declined, feeling annoyed at her for making me feel like a little boy. *I will fix that*, I thought, *as soon as I walk and drive. Gosh, why does everything take so long to happen for me?*

Ms. Molly was standing in the doorway welcoming me, and the rest of her family was right behind her. Two men lifted my chair up the two steps and wheeled into the living room. There I was introduced to a bunch of grown-ups.

The questions seemed to have no end until Angela came to the rescue, saying, "Leave the man alone. He has not been around such a big bunch of roughnecks."

She took control and wheeled me to the garden and feeding stalls around the house. I missed the smells of the farm and wondered where they kept the manure. Everything looked so clean. I noticed some machinery and a tractor that interested me.

"I know," Angela said, "you want to drive that." She pointed to the new red toy. "Don't worry, you will. But I hear Mom calling. It is lunchtime." Back with the crowd, she said, "George, I need to help in the kitchen." With that, she left me, and I rolled myself through the house.

I was amazed how roomy and wheelchair friendly all the rooms were. The dining room had a table with twelve oak chairs and one enormous-looking hutch. Folks were standing around waiting for an invitation to sit.

"What kind of beer would you like?" Someone showed me a container filled with ice and various bottles of beer.

"I take a Heineken."

Everyone said a toast and bottles clang together.

"Welcome, George, to the family," Joe said. "Let's sit down."

I was rolled to the open area without a chair, and the familiar sound of home and moving chairs on the floor so noisily came to mind. I heard my mom shouting, "When will you learn to sit without making that racket?"

Angela's mom came with platters of cut-up chicken. I would have known her from anywhere; Angela looked just like her.

She came behind my chair, hugged my shoulder a little, and said, "George, you are no strangers to us. We know everything about you. Angela has been informing us. You are another hero, like so many men and women fighting out there. So I hope you feel at ease among us and will be part of the family."

I could barely say thank you because I felt overcome with emotion. The word *hero* touched a chord, wondering who the wounded were and which limbs they left in the sand. After prayer, it got really busy around me. So many well-meaning hands tried to fill my plate—folks talking, telling jokes, and teasing one another.

Angela was bringing and taking; she never sat down. *Was she eating in the kitchen? I wondered.* I couldn't stop eating. The aroma in my nostrils from the food was so delicious, and I remarked on the great taste of everything.

"You mean to tell me you don't get chicken over there?"

"Sure," I said. "I have no complaints, but this is different."

"Sure, it is. This is family," Ms. Molly said.

Someone shouted, "And grandma had a hand in preparing it."

So it went on until the strudel was placed on the table.

"Wait and see how you like that dish. George, you have never eaten better strudel. Here let me help you. Rum or vanilla sauce?"

"I don't know," inhaling the rum sauce.

"Well, try rum first and then vanilla."

"Oh God, this is really to die for."

"Isn't it? That is Ma's specialty, and you're the reason we're eating it on an ordinary Sunday."

"Well, thank you," I said, looking into the eyes of Angela's mom as she cocked her head a little and two blues smiled at me.

"That is right," she said.

The men talked about the new tractor, and Joe offered to take me for a ride if I wanted.

"Angela warned us to be gentle with George."

"Still, I think I should drive him around."

"No, you won't. That is a man's thing. Leave us be."

"George will tell us what to do. Let's go."

So I ended up on the tractor in no time; besides, Joe showed me all the new gadgets that come with an El Toro tractor. It was not easy to balance myself without feet on the ground, so the ride was very short and I was lifted back into my chair. The helpless feeling overcame me once more.

I tried to keep my pride by saying, "It won't be long before I will be walking.

"That's great! You'll come and visit with us anytime, you hear. I got to do some chores now, George."

"Yes, I know there is no day off when you are farming, I remember."

"You are right, the world needs food, and we love our farm life."

Joe rolled me back to the house. Angela was sitting on the steps, waiting to take me back to the center.

"I had a great day, Angela. Thanks so much."

"Good, I guess you are tired and ready for a nap."

"Right you are. I still feel so full. Gosh, I ate so much more then I usually do."

Angela said, "Fresh air and different scenery can do that to us. As long as you enjoyed my folks, that is all that matters."

"Here we are, walking me to my room, I said."

"You know, George, I will do the same, having a nap when I get home."

"Good idea. Thanks again, dear, for a very special day."

A kiss on my cheek, a wave of her hand, "See you, George," and I was alone. I got myself on the bed as my body felt tired all over.

If you cam dream
it, you can do it
`Walt Disney`

CHAPTER 16

*hat a day I had, looking at the pictures on the wall, seeing
my siblings at home doing the same thing every Sunday as
I experienced today. So many miles apart and such resem-
blance between the two households—it's amazing*, I thought.

I must have fallen asleep because I heard the gong for dinner. I
was not hungry but I got up, and as I wheeled to the dining room,
I asked about the fellows who had arrived overnight. I wondered
whether I could visit with them.

Not being hungry, I waited in the hall, and after a while, I was
told, "No, George, you cannot."

I wondered why and dared to take the elevator to the intensive
care area. The hall was long and wide. It felt so quiet, and one could
not hear footsteps. Still, nurses were moving in and out of large double doors. Two men in green came walking toward me. They asked
what they could do for me.

"Nothing," I said. "How are the wounded from last night?"

"Are you related?"

"Yes and no, they are my buddies."

"Visitors are not allowed in this area. The men are resting. That
is all the information we can give you at this time."

Father Paul rushed by. "Later, George, I am busy now."

I sat unable to move and felt this unpleasant aggravation taking over. I used to feel this way all the time when I was helpless and
hostile toward the world. Yet I met such good people today. *Total
strangers inviting me to be family, just think about it, George. What
could be better?*

So why do we have to have wars? Why does the world not see that all this suffering was brought on by those warmongers, those greedy few who created war and tried to feed us lies, the reasons for wars to defend our country? Saddam Hussein. What did they call it the "Axis of Evil"? As I see it, Bush was exploiting our fear and mentioned the possibility of the devastating invasion of Iraq; therefore, we needed to destroy them first. "Defend our country." Lies, nothing but lies, I thought.

What do we know of what these men are going through in the ICU? What about family, children, or girlfriend or boyfriends? They are resting and waiting for results. What bull the public is told!

I ended up in the chapel. The evening sun shone into one window especially bright. I recognized Jesus walking on water, inviting Peter to come out of the boat to join him. Peter was afraid of taking the invitation. I forget, but Jesus mentioned something like "people of little faith."

As the chapel became darker, I was alone with the eternal light—not flickering, just steady, faithfully burning for all who wanted to be here. My brain was working overtime, thinking of everything, from school coming up to when I might be walking independently, from the events of the day to the men who where fighting to stay alive out there in the sand and here in the intensive care unit. I could not focus on a prayer.

"Oh God," I said, "you know what I want to say, Creator. Make me understand the world and where I belong in this mess."

"Here you are, George. No supper for you?" Father Paul said. He sat on the steps, looking up at me. "How was your day? From what I hear, you are doing great and will be out of this chair in a week or so."

Looking at him, I said, "Please, no small talk. How are the men who arrived last night?"

"Fighting for their lives at the moment, just as you did not so long ago, George. But it's time to go to bed."

I almost missed therapy next morning.

"What's going on in your life, George?" Jim shouted.

"I got mail from home with a lot of pictures."

"OK, but put some energy into your work here first. Your walk is not on autopilot yet, and you need to concentrate on every step, George. This is very important right now. You have lots of energy this morning. Great, want to try something new again?"

"I am ready," I almost screamed.

"Let us try to use crutches. Here, stand at the edge of the bar and turn around. Let's grab these while I hold you from the back. Wait, we have to see if these fit right."

"Looks good."

"Remember, your legs are strong and they will hold you. You must believe this, George. Move the right crutch in front with the right foot. Don't worry, I am here. You feel me holding you? Now the left. Don't look down. Look forward again, forward. Don't worry, I am here," Jim said, encouraging me.

Dr. Phillips shouted, holding her arms wide open to me, "What a great sight, George! You are doing it."

"Let's sit down, OK? Watch it, this can be tricky," Jim said.

"I am perspiring and shaking, Jim. Is that normal? My wheelchair, where is my wheelchair?"

"It's behind you. Pretty soon you won't need it anymore."

"What is this, are we on strike?" Dr. Kopp said, out of nowhere.

"Dr. Kopp, so good to see you," Jim said.

"Did you see me walk? I just finished walking with crutches."

"I saw a little as you were finishing, son," Dr. Kopp said.

He turned the wheelchair around a few times with me sitting in it.

"It's great to see you making progress," Dr. Kopp added.

I felt my heart filling with love for that man looking at him, smiling with his eyes right into my soul.

"Could you perform for me after you had this little booster?" Then he handed me a container of nutritive.

All three sat on the floor, looking up at me drinking the vanilla drink.

"It's good, thank you. What will it do for me?"

"Give you energy, George," Dr. Philips said.

"Haven't seen you for a while. What is going on, George?" Dr. Kopp asked. "Jim and Dr. Philips gave reports about your statuses in progress. What have you to contribute to that, George? Are you ready for school? You have two weeks to get on your feet. Soon, you will be very busy learning how to be my right hand. By the way, did you get your VA check as yet?"

"Yes, I did."

"George?" Dr. Phillips asked.

"That's not a good idea, buddy, leaving money laying on the bed. Have you thought of where you will live, George?" Dr. Kopp asked. "Dr. Philips mentioned you wanted to stay here in his room paying rent. Personally, I don't believe that is the right idea. You see, George, you need to detach yourself from this area," Dr. Kopp continued.

"You are going to be a private citizen and have no time to be concerned about your buddies here. This is the time for you to totally rehabilitate yourself, not only physically but mentally also. I understand the attachment you feel to your fellow comrades is great, but you will be helping them by becoming a success yourself first, George. This rehab is always open for you, and you will come here for therapy since you want to stay here in Germany."

"Yes, I do, and honestly, I really don't know how and where to begin. I am looking so forward to walking without crutches or the chair, being whole again. Yet at times, I feel I am freaking out and want to hide," I confessed.

"Yes, it is a big new world out there for you, George, but remember your friends, all of us here, will assist where we can. I hear what you are saying, and I understand your anxiety. It is like cutting Mother's apron string. It's like the bird—what is his name, bald eagle?—yes, Mother takes them for a ride on her wings, but when she thinks they should fly, she lets them fall and watches them and picks them up when she sees they are tired."

"It's the eagle," I said.

"You have that same security here, George. So go out there and be the best student you can be. Get a scholarship and run with it."

"We have faith in your ability," Dr. Philips said. Looking at her watch, she got up, patted my back, excused herself, and left.

"That's it," Dr. Kopp said. "George, remember, you don't ever have to feel alone. We are here for you all the way." Then he left too.

"Good session today," Jim said. "See you in the afternoon."

He left me sitting alone. *What now? Oh well, I might as well look if I have some money.*

CHAPTER 17

I looked at a brown envelope laying on the bed with a government stamp on it. Holding it in my hand, smelling it, turning it around, thinking, *Looks very impressive.*

My eyes saw the check with six numbers.

Wait a minute. That cannot be. The period must be wrong.

Then I looked at the numbers again. I took a pen and counted the numbers from the back. To be sure, I did it again.

Wow, I never had this much money in my life, I thought, holding the check in my hand. *But this is American currency. Up to now, I had not much to do with finances, but I was not a soldier anymore. I am a civilian living in a different country. Seriously, is this enough to support myself for a month?* I needed to know before I moved into an apartment.

Taking the elevator to the bank downstairs, the teller explained the difference between American and German money, saying, "Young man, you are losing one-third percent of your currency."

What to do? was my question. *Can I stay in Germany with this small pension?* Anyway, I opened up my first checking account. *Such helpful folks,* I thought on the way back to my room.

Passing by a bulletin board, I noticed an advertisement "Apartment for Rent." I called the listed number, and yes, it was available.

Angela, where are you when I need you?

Curiosity of wanting to know how much money I needed monthly, I took a taxi. Again, I was surprised by how helpful even taxi drivers were. He helped me into the car and handled my chair. I gave him the address. The apartment I saw was downstairs, but the one for rent was upstairs.

Too bad, I thought. *It's in walking distance to school, and I figured that I might just squeeze by financially.*

The taxi driver was waiting for me. He seemed to know what I was after and asked me about what I had seen. I explained my needs. He listened attentively and explained that I was late hunting for a living space, saying most apartments close to school were rented by then.

Also needing to be on ground floor was another factor of not getting anything more reasonable. He mentioned the positive aspects of living near school including that I would not need a car or insurance. Both of those meant big savings, and I should consider all points before making a decision.

It was a short taxi ride, and I considered walking home. I had so much to think about and felt energetic and confident in myself. I paid him.

"Here is my card," the driver said. "If it gets too hard to walk, call." He saluted me and drove away.

By God, it felt so good undertaking some action. I sat there alone in a strange country, thinking of all that happened in just two years in my life—tracing back the highs of pride sitting in the train then the lows of having lost my legs, wanting to take my life, and here again feeling on top of the world in a strange country, boasting with energy and confidence.

Looking down at my stumps that were shaking hard, I wondered what reasons I had to be in that jolly mood? Was it the money I had? I was still sitting in a wheelchair, dependent on people. "George!" I said out loud, "you are recovering."

On the way toward to the center, people greeted me, asking if I needed help. Others remarked on the weather, smiling at me as I smiled back. *Gosh, I haven't smiled for so long. This is truly a friendly town*, I thought. *George, you have made the right decision on staying here and beginning a new life, picturing a new future, with doors wide open to learn with a new vision.*

The emotion I felt was strong enough to lift me out of this chair. Oh, how fortunate I was. With gratefulness in my heart for all these blessings, I wheeled myself closer to home. This is the beginning of a new life.

Everything happened so fast, with not much time to think about my buddies still fighting for their lives in the fields so far away. How I wished that all of them could see flowers, shrubs, and greenery and feel, for just a little while, the friendliness of the people.

Even though buildings were just brick and mortar, large, and mostly square, the balconies were covered with a glass wall from which colorful hanging planters were filled with greeneries and flowers. All this gave these square-looking buildings a friendly look. The wide walkways between the little gardens, with white painted benches to sit, added another attraction for folks to want to live in this neighbourhood.

There must be housing for guys like me around here somewhere, I thought. *This area is still close to school. It would be great to live here.*

Wheeling my body in this chair took a lot of energy. A little later, I strolled downstairs and found my buddy at McDonald's serving customers behind the counter.

"Hey, George! How is it going? Are you here to help me?" he asked.

"No, but I would appreciate a burger, when you're not busy."

"No problem. If you can wait for twenty minutes, I will close up and we can have one together."

"OK, I am going to do some window shopping."

The lights were turned off in many stores, and slowly I got back to the restaurant. Jess was making us a burger when I returned.

"I am paying, remember, Jess?"

"Don't be silly, George."

"Well, let me buy you a beer, Jess."

"OK, fair enough. If you will have one too."

I realized how hungry I was and truly enjoyed my food while sitting with a friend.

"You are quiet, George. What is happening in your life?"

"You know, Jess, I can't help thinking of the guys out there while I am so at peace and relaxed sitting here. It is so wonderful, and sometimes I feel guilty feeling so good. Just a few month ago, I felt afraid and angry all the time. If I had the opportunity, I would have killed myself. I felt the whole world was my enemy. No quiet time. When you were not watching out for yourself, you were watching out for your buddies."

We both stopped eating as though honoring the soldiers out there. I felt Jess's eye on me and knew he understood what I was talking about.

After a long while, he said, "You know, George, the best thing is to suppress these thoughts. It's been two years for me, and still I am fighting the stupidity of this war. Mark my words, George, we are creating an unrest for many years in these areas. They don't want us there, but we want that oil. That's it in a nutshell. Let's leave it at that. Drink your beer, it is getting late."

"Right," I said.

"I have to get ready for school this week and need to do some shopping beforehand. What about you, George? Are you making plans?"

"Yes, matter of fact, I enrolled in the first semester in nursing."

"That's funny. I was thinking about becoming a nurse myself when I came home. I wanted to be there for my buddies when they arrived wounded from the field. Then I was advised that I fit better in the business world. I don't know how my boss got that impression. I am taking accounting. I like these classes. They are interesting. Another year then I am done, and we will see. So, tell me, George, did you find that apartment?"

"Heck no. I just started to look today."

"You better get going because those houses close to school are being picked up quick around this time."

"Where do you live, Jess?"

"I live with my girlfriend on Charles Street. Her parents have a rooming house there. We both leave the house at seven. Emma goes to work and I to school. It works out fine."

"It sounds like you have your life planned, Jess. Are there any wedding plans in sight?"

"Hope so, George. I want to live back home in New Mexico, close to my folks, but Emma does not want to come unless we marry here first."

"Fantastic! Let's drink to that. To Emma and Jess."

"OK, George. I've got to close up. See you around. Good luck finding that apartment."

"Thanks! See you, Jess. So far, so good."

CHAPTER 18

"Getting pretty fast, strapping on that gear," Angela shouted, watching me from the doorway the next morning. "How are you George?"

"Good, good."

"Angela, where have you been?"

"Getting ready for school. Are you doing the same, George?"

"Trying to, but I need to find somewhere to live first."

"Oh, here comes Jim," she said. "I'll be back in an hour."

Jim realized that I was not at my best and asked what happened after I left yesterday.

"Nothing, Jim, really. I feel anxious looking for somewhere to live and getting ready for school. That is all."

"George, put everything out of your mind for now. We are going to train walking without mistakes and falling, understood?"

"OK," I said, wondering what got into him suddenly. "OK, I felt good walking the bar barely holding on," I told Jim.

"I noticed," he said.

"You want to try the cane?"

"Only one, Jim?"

"Up to you. I am right here, George."

"You know, I am really beginning to trust these prostheses, Jim."

"You can. They are your legs. I have confidence in you, George."

Looking into Jim's smiling eyes boosted the trust in myself.

"So, I am walking only with a cane?" I said.

"Wait a minute, I need to measure the height and adhere the cane to your needs. Now let me show you, George. It's just like the crutches. You move the right cane forward at the same time as the left leg."

"That's not so easy, Jim."

"Don't even think about it. Just walk, George, walk and look up."

"It works, it works." I walked up and down, from one end to the other, until Jim gestured me to sit down. He sat beside me.

"I can't believe it, Jim. I am walking."

"You are walking, George. Are you feeling good?"

"I cannot describe what I feel like Jim." I felt my eyes filling again, taking a deep breath, my hands feeling down my new legs, thinking that I was given a great gift. "I feel very grateful to you and all the professional help I received to be where I am now. Thanks a million, Jim."

I wanted to embrace him, but do I dare?

Jim apparently thought it to be OK two men hugging, embracing me, clapping his hands against my shoulders hard. Looking at each other with my eyes swollen with tears, he pointed to a chair and said, "You are a good student. Now, I need to explain something very important to you, George, and I want you not to forget what I am going to say.

"Your brain knows that you are walking. In a few days, if you don't think of the danger of falling, slipping, or turning too fast, you become careless about your new legs. You will be getting up walking, not giving a thought to be very careful not to fall. You must exercise caution with walking so you don't have an accident. Keep your mind on walking for a while.

"The slightest mishap would set you back a month of agonizing time loss, like pain, guilt, back to the beginning with practice, and even refitting. Walking with caution should be your number one thought for some time. It is like driving a car. One needs to concentrate on driving. I know you have to get ready for school, but whatever you do, the most important thing is walking without falling. See you this afternoon, George."

"George, listen to Jim."

"Angela! Where did you come from? You want me to show you what I did? Won't take but a minute," I begged.

"Take it step by step. When you walk, think only of walking."

"OK, OK. I won't forget, Jim." Thinking, *I heard it now for the emptiest time.*

Sitting beside me, Angela pulled out a little card and gave it to me. "For you," she said.

"How come? It's not my birthday."

"It will be soon, we know. I just could not wait. Open it, dear." She smiled.

It was so flat and small. I wondered what the gift might be. This little, hard cardboard read, "Welcome to the Computer World."

"Open more, George. A gift card for your computer."

I just looked at her. "What does it mean?"

"Goodness, you are slow this morning. Sorry, I should not have said that, George. It's a gift to buy a computer from all of us. Come on. Let's go shopping for it."

I did not know how fast we arrived downstairs, but Angela seemed so happy as if it was her gift.

"I don't know anything about computers," I said.

"You'll learn. They have special classes for you right here in the store."

The clerk mentioned three different models. Angela said, "The best is Microsoft. That is what I have."

"OK, here is the newest we have," the clerk said.

Looking at the price, I quickly said, "I don't like it. I could not accept such a gift."

"Don't be silly, George. You don't even know what you like." She motioned to have it set up so that we could play with it. After sitting with Angela learning, repeating, and trying things that can be done with a computer for an hour, I felt tired but so very amazed of what could be done with a computer.

Looking at me smiling, she said, "Do you like it now, George?"

"Yes, I do. Let's get out of here," I quickly said.

"Wait a minute. We must get the accessories first."

Taking a deep breath, I said, "Angela, it was fun, but I will not accept such an expensive gift."

"You are so bloody stubborn, George. You know how we all feel about you. If I tell them you won't accept our gift, you will hurt the feelings of the family. Do you understand that? We all chipped in, knowing that your birthday is just two weeks from now. So what is the big deal?"

"Angela, let me think. You are so fast with everything. Let me take you out for a hot dog."

"OK, George, but promise me you will not make a fuss and just show happiness for the friends that you have."

I thanked the clerk for her time and mentioned that we will return.

"You are welcome, Mr. Reynolds."

"Mister?"

"How did she know my last name, Angela?"

"I told her your name."

I hoped Angela did not see my tears, but nothing goes by that woman. So she stepped in front of me, giving me a Kleenex saying, "Don't you know, George? We love you," and she planted a kiss on my nose.

"Thank you. You are crazy Germans, but I feel I don't deserve all that attention."

"Is it not amazing how good a hot dog tastes when you are hungry, George?"

"And when you are with a lovely woman," I ended up saying.

"So, what else do you need, George?"

"I have no idea."

"Didn't you do any shopping?"

"No, I don't know what I need, Angela. I am anxious to get into an apartment, possibly furnished and close to school so I can walk to my classes."

"Did you check the bulletin board today?"

"No, but yesterday."

"Let's go look today."

"I have an address from the one yesterday but did not look at it because I got too tired."

"You want to do that now?"

"OK, but I need a rest before therapy, Angela."

"OK then. We do it after your exercise so you can have your rest now. I will walk you to your room. I'll practice the organ for a bit and pick you up at around 4:00 p.m."

I fell on the bed and slept for an hour. When I woke, I brushed my teeth and made it in time for Jim. I did not dare tell him about my exciting morning. He probably would be giving me a lecture again for not thinking walking. I understood he meant well. The damage from falling could set me back.

Remembering what he had warned me about so many times, "Your success is my success," and yes, I respect him for his concern. So I walked with one cane. We practiced sitting and getting up from chairs with various heights. It was not easy, and without having Jim at my side, I could not do it. The cane was in my way frequently.

What do people do who use canes? I wondered. I will save that question for another time. Apartment hunting was on my mind.

"That is Great, George. One more time around, and I'll let you go."

Feeling a boost of satisfaction from these few compliments of Jim, I did this last round eagerly.

But the cane fell on the floor.

"Try to pick it up, George. I am right here."

"Nothing to it," I said. Trying to reach down and Jim watching me was another matter I just could not do.

"Do you need it, George?"

"Well, to tell you the truth, I feel better with it."

Angela was standing at the door. She let out a "Hallelujah," opened her arms wide, and I walked right into them without the cane. We stood close together. I had not realized that Angela was so much shorter than me. I used to have to look up from the chair. Standing in front of her being tall, looking into her blues, oh boy. I had no words for that feeling.

My cane fell on the floor again. I had to hold on something, fast. So I held her instead of her bending to hold me. I felt her body moving closely into mine. I did not want to let go of her. I wanted to hold on to the exhilarating, awakening new feelings.

Angela stepped back just holding my hands, saying, "How wonderful! How great, you are free of the chair. Let me look at you, George." She quickly moved back to me, holding me. "You are so tall," she said.

"And you are so small, Angela."

We all laughed. I was standing free of equipment, not even the wheelchair behind me. Jim picked up the cane and gave it to me.

He brought the chair to me and said, "It might be better to keep it for a few more days."

"Good idea." I nodded my head with approval.

"Try walking with Angela in the chair."

In no time she sat, waiting for me.

"Let's go see Grandma."

"Too far," Jim intervened. "Let's just go around the room once, George."

Holding on to the chair, I was glad Jim was right besides me.

My fear vanished. I had my security blanket—Jim walking beside me.

Angela hopped out of the chair before she applied the brakes.

"Not so fast," I said while the chair moved forward.

Jim grabbed me under my arms, noticing the chair was going to fast. "Please, no hero play," he said, pointing a finger at Angela.

"Let's go and show Grandma you standing without help," Angela said. "Did you not hear what Jim just said?"

"I know, I know. Maybe you just could stand up with the cane."

"George is too uncertain without me. Wait a few days before trying to do things without me, Angela."

"You are right, Jim. Who would pick him up in case of falling?"

"Let's go see the apartment first. I am anxious. I need a home, Angela."

The sun was warm, but clouds were moving in faster than we thought.

The owner of the building looked at Angela then me, saying, "You were here yesterday. I have good news. In a week, a smaller unit would open downstairs. It might need some painting and repairing.

Let me check whether you can see it. The young lady is in. I will ask if you could see it."

I looked around, seeing that the location was nice. Toward the back, Hans, the owner, returned with a young woman, Anita, who greeted us with a big smile on her face, telling us that she was getting married.

"Yes, yes, you can move in next week. Do you need any furniture?" she asked. Walking toward the open door, she turned and said, "Don't worry, I have it all cleaned."

I noticed the large window. I was sold right there and then. It had a lovely view to a back garden. There was so much clutter on the furniture and bed, but it did not matter; I wanted to live here. I could decide on furniture later.

"How much is the rent in euros?" Without hesitating, I wanted to pay the first month's rent without having looked at the bathroom.

I noticed Angela hesitating on my quick decision, and she asked if we could think about it until morning.

"Sure," Hans said. "Anita just told me this morning of her moving. If you return tomorrow, I don't have to advertise."

It was pouring rain now, and Hans suggested that we sit on the covered porch in the backyard. We sat and listen to the rain a moment. I felt like my heart would burst any moment, being so lucky.

"Look at this, Angela. I love it. Behind is my window. I have a great view."

"I agree. It's very nice and so private."

I noticed that Angela's hand was resting on my arm. I liked that feeling and didn't move, afraid she might pull her hand away.

"Let's go. Maybe Grandma is still at the library," she said. "Let me wheel you home."

"I can do it myself, Angela, I did it yesterday."

It was still sprinkling, but the air was warm. We ended up walking in the rain to the center. *Simply heaven*, I thought. It was dark in the library. Evening was approaching.

"It's been a big day for you today, George."

"Yes," I agreed, "a lot of things have happened, and I feel it in my bones."

"OK then. If you want me to come by tomorrow, we can play with your new toy, if you like."

"What do you think about the apartment. Should I take it?"

"It is your decision, George. The price is right, there are some pieces of furniture you can get for a reasonable price, but the main thing is, you can walk to school."

"Very true, Angela," I said, nodding. "I will go and pay the rent."

"Great! I will see you tomorrow then." She kissed my cheek, and gone she was.

Mm, why is this woman always in a hurry leaving me? I thought. *Just wait, my friend, pretty soon you won't be bending down to kiss me. You will have to tiptoe.*

For a moment, I relived that great satisfaction of being a man standing tall in front of Angela. The mirror on the back wall showed me sitting in that ugly chair. I had the urge to stand up by myself, holding onto the wall. *Should I try against Jim's approval?*

CHAPTER 19

"Hi, buddy. Are you waiting for someone, or can I walk with you to dinner? It's ribs tonight."

"Sounds good, let's go then. I'm hungry too."

"What have you been doing lately? I have not seen much of you, George."

"I see you are taking your cane. That is smart, using it before you get too tired."

"I walked around behind the wheelchair. I just was not ready to give it up," Jacob said.

"Some smart-ass hid it from me one night, and I had to walk to therapy. Guess who it was? You are right. It was Jim himself. He new what he was doing, I guess."

"Glad you told me that, Jacob."

"I hated that bloody wheelchair, and yet I felt insecure when I did not have it close to me. Those guys are great over there, all of them, I must say."

"I agree with you on both accounts. I wish I had the patience they have. Here comes our chow. Smells good."

"Let's eat," I said.

It was quiet; just the clicking and clanging of the utensils was heard for a while.

I was occupied with thoughts about my walking like a normal person, realizing that maybe life was worth living and my future was in the making. *Open doors.*

My thoughts crossed the ocean. I had forgotten that I was the tallest at home. My mom would say, "Just like his uncle Jack." I never met the man. Wondered what other DNA traits I inherited from him.

I felt good about myself this evening. Realizing that I was tall and not bad to look at gave me confidence, and I could not help thinking of Angela not having to bend down. With great satisfaction, I relived that moment once more standing much taller in front of Angela. After dinner, Jacob and I called it a day. It had been a bustling day, reminiscing with some thoughts of fulfilment of these important events.

I will really like the apartment. I forgot to ask if the kitchen was furnished. I was hasty, realizing that I did not know anything about the kitchen. *If I have to buy all that stuff, food too eat, wash my clothes, and get good grades, I will be a busy guy for sure.* I was thinking for the first time, I need to take care of myself. *Not my mom, not the army, but I—I have to do it for myself. You have to be smart, not waste time or money. Scary.* So I prayed.

Weeks flew by, Grandma Molly and Angela had been there for me all the way. My apartment became so comfy. The fridge was full of ready-to-eat stuff and easy-to-prepare food. Hans, the owner, was also computer informed and booted my computer up and showed me around.

Jim and Dr. Phillips had visited me, actually walked with me one morning to school and then to the cafeteria. I had no fear of walking without the chair or cane. I was rehabilitated and praised by both.

Dr. Philips reiterated, "Remember, when times seem difficult, George, come home and talk with us. The next couple of years are going to be a challenge for you."

Finally, I was alone, sitting in my favourite red chair that Hans found in the storage room. *This is just what a man needs,* I thought, *after a hard day's work.* There were a few dishes in the sink, but otherwise I kept my clothes hung up. I had done a lot of walking during the first couple of weeks, finding all my classes and confirming each schedule.

I wondered where Angela was hanging out. *Was this school that large that we would not meet? I had not seen or heard from her. I must have fallen asleep, the second night in a row.* I blamed it on the red chair. I realized the danger of how quickly a guy like me could get in trouble and procrastinate, getting behind in schoolwork.

I understood my counsellor, Mrs. Hemlock, advising me not to get sidetracked by anything. She said, "Just get adjusted to schoolwork, since it has been some time since you have been in school."

This special concentration had to be relearned. I explained that I had just learned to walk without the cane and how my trainer advised the importance of keeping my mind on walking for a while. Funny, it was just like in the olden days when my mom put her foot down when I looked longingly out wanting to be with my friends playing. *I have to become my own thought.*

Standing in front of a mirror, looking at myself, I thought, *Not so bad in slacks that covered my prostheses.* Removing them and standing on my stumps was problematic in that anger found its way to my brain and the old fury of government's rules wanting to interfere with my new way of thinking.

"George! This is history. Forward, George, deal with the now. Think of the many graces you have received," I said out loud.

On the first school day, it was raining, more like drizzling. I enjoyed walking through the fog. The new shirt kept me warm; therefore, there was no need for rushing. I paid special attention to Jim's advice.

"You think that walking in the rain makes you more handsome?" Angela called through the window, waving at me to jump in. "Hi there, George, so nice to see you. All is well?"

"Thanks. All is well, Angela."

Regretfully, in no time, I was in front of the entrance to the class. Getting out of the car was not quite as easy as getting in. Angela jumped out to help, and there we stood together again like that morning at therapy.

Gosh, that feeling, I can't explain it.

Instead of tiptoeing, she bent my face down and placed a soft kiss on my cheek. Then she whispered, "Love you. Too-da-loo." She laughed and was gone, leaving me with my unexplained emotion, standing in the rain.

Even after she was gone, I felt her firm hand on the back of my neck while walking into class. I couldn't help thinking, *Damn it. She is playing games with me.* But I wanted desperately to hold on to her. *How, George, how? You have nothing to offer as yet. That will change. Just wait, that will change*, I promised myself.

First session was a spelling test. Ms. June wanted to know our abilities. I could not understand what spelling had to do with nursing. I was not the only person thinking that way. We were told the importance of knowing to how to write nursing reports accurately, but it did not make sense to me. Well, I had gone over some vocabulary in the first ten pages in the book and felt confident remembering some. My English grades satisfied Mom and Dad during high school. To learn how to speak German was a whole lot different.

When I tried the little I had learned with some nurses, they smiled kindly and quickly spoke English with me. When I mentioned this to my German teacher she explained, "Well, it's either they know you are a GI and want to be helpful, or they want to practice their English. But any time you wish to speak German, come to me. I am interested in knowing you better, George.

I felt a blush coming on and said "Thanks" and left. She is pretty but much older than I.

Anatomy and physiology seem interesting subjects but will be difficult to master. I probably spend much time in these books. Knowing the function of the organs, bones, muscles, circulation, and more, I had my doubts about being able to keep my grades up in these two important classes

The Search for Meaning in Life is the last book and class of the day. In this book, we are to read a collection of various authors. I will enjoy essays that make me think of what the authors believe. Another essay by William James, "Is Life Worth Living?" describes the positive contribution of religious faith on making an effective living compared to science, which cannot provide that essentiality. It is the last class, and I walked home, wondering how little human life meant to the warmongers in the world.

I am studying the worth of humanity, yet world leaders use young people as canon fodder, fighting and shooting for monetary things. This

is a global human frustration. Who is the questioner in all this turbu-lence? I had no answer to all this. It's like Mother said, "War has been around hundreds of years before us and will be hundreds of years after us."

This puzzle has no answer.

No time to ponder on that heavy subject. I have to study on the gen-eral body structure—in other words, what our body is made of. I better get home and become better informed.

It had stopped raining; the air so fresh and the smells of garden greens and flowers made the walk home a delight. I settled down at the kitchen table, opened my anatomy textbook, and read about the body. It's amazing how we are put together, and people rarely think anything about it. It is all gratis, a gift of the Creator God. *How great thou art*, I thought.

It was 9:30 p.m., and I had not eaten. I searched the fridge and found a box saying "Grandma's stew." Just the right stuff. I was hungry. While I was enjoying the meat, I was wondering how we were asked questions on test. *Did she say it was multiple choices? I had forgotten. I better not watch TV tonight and hop into bed early. I need to do well tomorrow.*

If there was anything I hated in this new life of mine, it was taking off the prosthesis. Not like other folks' socks and shoes—no, I am taking off my legs. How terrible. My whole life, I have to take off my legs and walk on my stumps. I realized that I turned off the lights. *No wonder. Who wanted to see this cripple? What kind of woman would want to live with me?*

It had happened so fast I gave my oath to loyalty and obedience to the American army when I enlisted. For that, I wanted to be edu-cated in foreign affairs, travel, and be somebody. *Well, George, you cannot blame anybody whether you believe this war is justified or not. It is you who signed up. Hell, I know. I can still make the best of it, and I do have the opportunity to do so. Get on with it, George.*

Next morning, we were handed two pages of sentences. We were to read them through then place the right word in the appro-priate space.

"If you have questions about what they mean, let me now and we can discuss them," the teacher told us.

Next class, the test was multiple choices. There were forty of them, to be done in one hour.

"You can leave when you are done. Please do not discuss the test with others here in class."

Orders, orders. This is murder, I thought. I felt anxious as I had problems understanding the questions and finding the best answer for the first ten questions, but then I settled in and actually enjoyed that hour. I finished just in time, and I was the last one out of class.

"How do you think you've done, George?" Ms. Bauer asked.

"You will be the first one to know," I said, returning her smile.

So one day turned into a week, and weeks turned into months without doing anything but study. Too bad there was only one Sunday in the week because I usually ended up at Grandma Molly's house for dinner and was given leftover food that lasted for a few more days. I was grateful for that. It felt like home; these folks showed me how Christianity should be lived like. It's difficult to explain because I still felt anger and hostility, but this environment was sheer healing and stabilizing. *Yes, food for my dark soul.* Also, I saw Angela, we discussed school, and she showed me stuff on the computer.

Grandma asked, "What did you hear from home?"

I was perplexed. Funny, I had not thought of home at all. Well, that was not acceptable, and something needed to be done at once. In no time, I was given the receiver and talking with my mother.

"Son, I was so worried. Are you all right? You know it is 9:30 p.m. here and bedtime for us."

Well, we quickly forgot the time difference, and we talked. I had not realized my tears falling free until I saw the Kleenex that someone handed to me. She mentioned the baby girl smiling all the time and being spoiled by all of us and being handed from arm to arm during meals.

I asked about Peter my youngest brother and Ella my horse.

"Well, Ella is having a hard time now, lots of rheumatism in her legs. Peter has taken over loving him but does not want anything to be done to him." No, Peter, he is out. He has a girlfriend. Her name is Ann."

"Goodness, Mom, wait a minute. How old is he?" I asked.

"Yes, time flies, son."

Suddenly, the urge to see everybody came over me, and I promised that maybe I would come home after my first semester.

"Love you, Mom. Say hi to everybody." *Gosh, what had I said?*

Angela had apparently listened and popped the question, "Could I come too?"

Mentioning that she would be done and be an RN, deserving of a vacation, I did not know what to say. I was so full of questions that I forgot to ask Mother some other things.

Ms. Molly came to sit beside me, taking my hand into hers, saying, "From now on, you need to talk with your folks weekly, George. Your mother must have been worried sick."

"I am sorry. There has been so much change in my life, I totally forgot my family and my buddies at rehab."

"What you need is a phone that you carry so you can be in touch with the rest of the world," Angela mentioned. "I'll do the dishes, and we can go see what we can find."

"Run along, girl. I will do your dishes."

"Thanks, Grandma." She placed a kiss on her right cheek, and I did the same to her left one. Our eyes met for a long look, and then we embraced Grandma.

"You are truly the greatest," she said as she patted my back. "Run along, son, have fun."

I felt another squeeze, and Angela and I left.

We drove into town. There was little to say until she stopped the car at a Bell store.

"This is as good as any. What do you say, George?"

I looked at prices first, while Angela found the same cell phone she was using.

"Free."

"How come?" I asked.

"Well, you have to sign a two-year contract and pay so much monthly. That is what I do, and then you upgrade to a newer one."

I was holding this tiny device, capable of doing so many things. I ended up taking it home with me.

"Don't worry. I will help you, George. Let's go see your buddies. While you visit, I will practice the organ."

"OK, Angela, whatever."

From the chapel, I walked through the halls, the same ones that I hated not too long ago, remembering my anger and fury. I ended up sitting in the back of the chapel and listened to Angela practice and sing. She ended with, "There is someone who loves every soldier. He is only a prayer away."

I had come a long way in such short time, I thought. God, with your blessings, I might still have the chance to become a great individual, the kind that is needed in order to make this world a peaceful one. My grateful feelings of having met so many hardworking men and woman in this hospital, I declared them all heroes in my mind. Yes, I had been given a chance to belong to them.

"Father Paul, where did you come from? I have not seen you for some time," I said.

"Same here," he said, shaking my hands and then grabbing my shoulders.

Seated beside me now, he said, "I hear you are doing great, and you are looking great too. Private life must be good to you."

"So it is," I said. "And I am very busy with school."

"What did I tell, George? All is falling into play. Just keep the faith. We have to keep in touch. Let's have your phone number. I cannot stay to chat, I have to make some visits."

"I knew that I could not go into the unit where the new soldiers were being treated. Therefore, I did not ask—I promised to pray.

"Great, George, keep it up."

Again and again, feeling gratitude, it just popped up. Sitting here, I felt the love given to me from so many people, folks whom I did not know. I noticed it in so many different little ways. For instance, when I try to struggle speaking German, facial expressions turn into a smile, "You are doing great, buddy," even though I know I stumble.

It seemed everybody was a buddy in this town, but Grandma Molly topped it all. She is love and lives love. Suddenly, I needed to do something right then. *Was that the spirit talking with me?*

When Angela came, I asked her to drive me to a flower shop where I bought the biggest bunch of roses. I couldn't get to the farm fast enough. I just had to hug her and tell her that I love her.

"You are nothing but a softy yourself, George, just a wonderful young man. Someday, you will make a woman very happy. I hope I get to see it happen," she said.

I drove home, feeling satisfied with the day's end. Angela drove quietly without interrupting my thought. I thanked her for understanding my needs of showing grandma my gratitude being so good me.

CHAPTER 20

*O*n the first day of school at the end of September, I walked to class, and a brisk wind from the east reminded me that summer was about to end. I wished that I had dressed warmer, remembering not having any warm-ups meant another errand I had to take care of in the near future. I was looking forward to taking the bus, getting to know my adopted town. Of course, it had to wait until the end of the week.

I noticed Ursula waving to me from a bench on my way home. Coming closer, she pointed to the seat beside her; but I didn't want to show my difficulties of getting up. I excused myself that I had an appointment. So she got up and walked with me to the corner.

"Doing anything special tonight?" she asked.

"Yes," I said, "I am entertaining three special guests in my apartment."

"In that case, have fun." She turned around and left me. I wondered what she was thinking, who my guests would be. It was no lie; these books would be my special guests for the semester. A phone rang during my studies; I did not know at the moment that it was my cell phone.

"What took you so long to answer, George?"

"Sorry, Angela, I didn't realize it was my cell phone. You are the first person to call me."

"What are you doing tonight?"

"I am sitting with my three friends, here at the kitchen table. Would you like to join me?"

"No, it is too late tonight, maybe some other day."

I heard her chuckle, and she wished me a good night. The weekend came fast, and so did the cooler weather.

On Saturday morning, as I had planned, I ventured via bus to the city. Buses ran frequently, and I did not have to wait long. I had great difficulties stepping up the steps. The lady behind me said, "Ja [yes], these are very high here. Let me help you."

It was the first time that I experienced a problem with my prostheses. The driver mentioned the same problem with elderly folks and excused himself for not getting up to help.

"We are not supposed to get out of our seat when the motor runs," he explained.

After a short ride, getting out was easier, but I still I felt a little unsure. I looked around the first few minutes to get my bearings walking in strange territory. *Lots of people shopping today.*

I noticed a different atmosphere wandered through an open street market—vendors selling flowers, others offering all kinds of breads and sweets, and coffee bars served in all kinds of mugs, even very dainty demy cups. The strong aroma of coffee weakened. I just had to have a cup and be part of that weekend feeling. *Yes, that's what it is. It's the end of the workweek.*

Of course, I treated myself with a piece of coffee and *kuchen*— "cake" in German. I could sit here all day watching folks greeting and exchanging smiles. The only thing was, I needed to get up for another java. At home, the waitress would come to you and refill your cup. In Germany, one has to pay for the second cup.

Mother would have liked walking around here, I thought. *She did not mention that she had been in town. But where else did she buy the gifts for the family? My mother! Leaving her beloved farm, spending six weeks at my bedside, helping me getting out of my barrel of rot. Mom, with your prayers, I will become the man I said I'd be, when I left home. Sitting here in a foreign country, loving the moments of all the hustle and bustle of Saturday morning, was just great, and one day, Mom, I will treat you to enjoy a weekend morning with me.*

The thought of being able to do that gave me great enjoyment. A sudden hush of wind giving me a chill, reminding me of my reasons for being here. I got up and started walking, looking for a clothing store.

"Where will I find a sweatshirt?" I asked a clerk.

She pointed to a thrift shop across the street, telling me that in that store, I could find some reasonably priced ones.

Do I look like a poor man? I wondered. I walked over to the other side, realizing there were no cars driving or parked on the street. *What a smart idea for pedestrians young or old not having to rush. After all, it was Saturday—a day of rest. Great psychology*, I thought.

I had no problem finding a warm button-up shirt. I tried it and liked it, wearing it to the cash register.

The clerk said, "That is better. Thirty-five euros, bitte [please]." She noticed I felt cold when I came in.

Folks are so observing, it's amazing, I thought.

I was enjoying the walk to the bus stop, feeling warm and having adopted the mood of the weekend too. To complete it, I needed a pot of those big, fancy chrysanthemums. I held a yellow one in the air to take home. *But then, how am I getting onto the bus?* I thought. *I will look so foolish.*

The elderly woman held her hand open and looked at me. "Five euros, bitte."

"OK, you win." So I paid the smiling vendor and was the owner of a pot of flowers.

A young woman offered to hold on to the flowers while I climbed in the bus. Everywhere I looked, I noticed smiles. Was I silly or crazy carrying a pot of flowers around? People might think girlfriend, wife birthday, whatever—this happy-looking pot of green was just for me. Maybe it will keep my spirit up all week.

My chrysanthemums came home with me, looking great on the table. To finish up my day, I had lunch with some buddies in rehab. Feeling some pain in my left thigh, I wondered if that could have been from walking. *Might as well see Jim for a spell while I am here.*

So many buddies had left, and it seemed like a whole new group of men were occupying the dining room. Server Nancy recognized me and called me to sit at a table with two men.

"This is George," she said. "He was here for a long time, and look at him now. George, meet Bill and John."

"Great, you ended up in the best place to get well. I am George. You mind if I have lunch with you? That pizza smells good."

No one spoke, sitting down, but I felt eyes from the side looking at me. Bill had his face deep in his plate; an inch lower and he could have eaten without utensils. John sat up very straight as if he had a board under his shirt. Nancy brought a large piece of hot, freshly made pizza, and she remembered even the parmesan shaker. I offered some pizza around.

"Sure," John said, "I'll have some more."

Bill shook his head. "No thanks." He was still not looking up.

John shuffled his piece as fast as he could and, without saying another word, got up and walked out.

Finishing my slice, I wondered what had happened to John, looking around for him.

"Don't worry about that guy," Bill said, still his face in the plate. "He not only has a broken spine, he suffers from a broken mind also."

"What do you mean, Bill?"

"Wait until you hear him talk. You will know what I mean."

Finally, Bill finished his lunch and straightened out just a little and looking at me, saying, "You look too healthy to be here. What part of the body did you give to Uncle Sam?"

"I left my two legs in the sand and a couple of my buddies."

"Sons of bitches, sending us in that hellhole," Bill said. "I wonder if any of their sons are fighting over there." He looked at me with fierce, angry eyes, shaking his head wildly, appearing maniacal.

"Christ, what happened to you, Bill?"

"Yep. Take a good look at me. I am going crazy with pain and itches. My face is itching, but I was told to leave bandages off for a few hours daily to dry my skin. I hate to eat alone, but then coming out here, I have to put up with guys like you."

"What in heaven's do you mean 'guys like me'?" Not waiting for an answer, I said, "So sorry, man. You must have gone through hell, and how can one not stare?"

"Don't worry, I am getting used to the Stares. I can live with my burnt body, but with a face like this, I don't know, man. If I had a gun, I would shoot myself and everything around me."

"I hear you, Bill. Not so long ago, I felt the same and probably would have gone through with it."

After some time, Bill said, "I am told that after the third surgery, my face will look normal. I am so tired of being cooped up in my room, but coming out here is no fun either."

I had a tough time looking at his scarred face. We sat quietly for a while, except for Bill's fingers were busy imitating writing on a typewriter.

"Can I take you for a walk?" I finally asked.

"OK, get me out of here." His fast response startled me because he indicated before that he did not want to be seen in public.

"Let's tell your nurse or someone first," I said.

"No, no, I don't need permission. It's OK." He wiggled in his chair frantically. "Let's go, George."

I was looking for the brakes at the side of his chair and noticed a bell, but I did not give it any thought.

Nancy returned and asked if we wanted dessert. Bill suddenly became hostile, screaming at me for being a stupid so and so. Nancy wasted no time in calling Bill's nurse. Vivian showed up right away.

"Well, look who is here. George, my boy, you look wonderful." Vivian opened her arms wide for a hug. "And I see Bill found a friend."

I noticed how quickly Bill tilted his face down, cursing, mumbling four-letter words.

"Bill wants to go for some fresh air," I said, not sure if I still wanted to take him at this point.

"Sure, but right now, the doctor wants to see him," Vivian said and turned his chair to leave.

Bill started to scream, moving his body to get at Vivian, spitting and scratching whatever and however he could prevent from going with her. I heard him scream all the way down the hall. I sat down again, choked by all I just experienced. Nancy joined me and started to tell Bill's sad story.

"You know, George, Bill is suicidal. He's tried frequently since he has been here."

Another case of unbearable tragedy. When is it going to stop? I thought. *When, when is it going to stop?* I wanted to scream it out for the world to hear.

The day had begun great; too bad it ended in the gutter.

Vivian returned and sat with me.

"Sorry," she said, "but Bill is very strong and extremely hostile. I had to medicate him. Otherwise, I could not handle him."

"Is that the only way to medicate him, Vivian?"

"Yes, whenever he needs it," Vivian said. Patting my hand, looking at me, she said, "I remember you and many others acting just like Bill when you came. It takes time to let go off the mental stress that you folks go through. Bill was in isolation for a long time because of his burns. We wanted to save as much skin as possible to fix his face. There was so little of his face left and little skin left on his body that we could use. He is just plain tired, George, just tired of suffering."

"How can I help him? Do you think I could visit him? I mean, I don't have much time with school and all, but he needs someone."

"I will talk with his attending nurses, George."

"OK then, can I say good night to him now?"

"I'll go with you."

There he was, lying in bed, hands tied away from his body. He seemed to be sleeping.

"What the hell is that? Why are his hands tied?" I blurted out

Hushing me to be quiet, Vivian explained, "Bill will scratch his face while he sleeps. He should not touch the new skin."

"Can I sit here so he is not alone when he wakes?"

"OK, do not loosen his hands, George. That is an order. Call when Bill wakes up."

I was glad for the window in the room. It was getting dark; the wind was still strong as I watched branches dance the dance of the free. I thought of my days and months on the frontline—no greens there of any kind. I remembered the heat in our combat suite. When a gust of wind was blowing, the hot sand blinded my eyes, so much so that I nervously cleared it as fast as I could, afraid I could miss something and be in danger. *Life of a soldier in Iraq*, I thought.

Whenever there was a quiet moment, like here sitting with a buddy, I wondered how I got there. Everything happened so fast. *Why was I killing anybody who made the wrong move?* Buddies here all have the same story, different images of experiences I had listened to from comrades who had been fighting in Iraq but all ended up the same.

The screams of Bill calling those bums woke me out of my own dreams. I stood up and grabbed the Call button in Bill's left hand.

"Bill, it's me George. You are safe. I just wanted to visit with you a little. Do you need something?"

"I can't reach the urinal," he said.

I see it hanging on the bedrail. "Can I put it in place for you?"

We looked at one another and started to laugh, then our eyes filled with tears, and we both cried. Here I was, standing over the bed of a buddy suffering from severe wounds brought on by a war we were fighting, a war that probably neither of us understood. *Did Bill run away from home thinking the same dreams as I? Or did Bill believe that he would or could save the United States from being invaded by hostile enemies?*

I saw Vivian standing at the door and waved her to come and take over the bedside activity. I wanted to stay and watch if Bill's hand would be untied, but she told me it was time for me to go.

Looking at her, she said, "I will walk you home in about fifteen minutes, if you want to wait."

As I walked out, a male nurse arrived to help Vivian to take care of Bill's needs. I stood in the hall and heard the two nurses explaining to Bill what they were doing.

"You know the routine, Bill. I love you, guy, and hate like hell to tie you down, but this is the only way from keeping you fingers out of your face."

"Please, please understand, dear," Vivian said in a pleading voice. "I am going home now, but Karl here will keep you company until you fall asleep."

I did not hear a peep from Bill, nothing. *What was he think-ing or feeling? Was Bill's anger the same anger as mine?* I remembered my fury, totally uncontrolled. I remember how I ran that wheelchair through the halls. Screaming seemed to help. Like in the field, we would scream and run. We were always glad to hear familiar voices of knowing we were still all together during these attacks. I hoped they used medication freely on Bill; sleep was my lifesaver, and I wished the same for my buddy.

"Let's go home," Vivian said, walking toward me.

It was dark outside, and the wind had died down a bit.

After a while Vivian said, "George, not so long ago, you were in the same boat. I prayed for you when you felt the world hated you. Give us a couple of weeks, and Bill will be better and feeling less trapped, just like you felt after a stretch. You had your mother watching over you when you wanted to do harm to whomever you met during your sleep. She was a great help for us nurses. Bill has no family, and his sitter was unavailable to tonight. That is why we have to keep his hands tied. We have enough night staff, but we never know what can happen.

"Should Bill wake during an emergency, we could not be with him right away, leaving a lot of time for him to damage his new skin. His body wounds are healing remarkably well, and we have enough skin to build his face, if he can stay out of it. Does that answer some of your questions, George?"

We were standing in front of my apartment now. I turned toward that small-framed woman who was all heart, and I realized the dedication of this person and the staff.

"You guys are doing such good work. Vivian, how do you do it?" Where do you get the patience from?" I asked.

I noticed her pulling out a Kleenex. Her eyes were full of tears, and then Vivian's head leaned against my chest while I put my arms around her.

"George, it is so very hard sometimes," she said, "watching these young men and women in their anguish and suffering."

I felt her body shaking and held her tight against me.

"You are heroes, all of you," I whispered. "Thank you for what you do."

"You see, George, why it is so great to see guys like you coming through such great problem and returning to a normal life? That makes it all worthwhile. It gives us renewed energy and patience to do all we can for the wounded coming home broken."

We sat on the bench behind my apartment. The stillness and soundless, fast-moving clouds repaired our souls.

"What the hell are we doing it all for I ask you, Vivian? Do you believe we should worry about being invaded or attacked by another country?"

She looked at me from the side and slowly said, "Yes, I think so. We the Western world have created so many enemies in various countries. I believe we could be attacked, just look at 9/11.

"If these countries were strong enough, maybe they would do us harm because they see *us* like the attackers. Yes, we claim that we help them to become democratic and help to reform their life. As I see it and hear what many wounded men tell me, those people don't want to be like us. Those people hate us. And, George, don't forget, we want the oil. That is the all-important matter—control of oil. For that, you and so many men and women come home bleeding."

I listened very carefully. *Could I be that wrong? What was the majority of Germans' thinking? If all thought the same as Vivian, why did they not fight that war?* I felt uncontrolled anger making its way to my gut and mind.

Vivian suddenly got up and shook me by saying, "Stop it, George. From now on, we are not discussing war anymore."

"Wait a minute. Just answer one thing for me. Can any war be justified? Look at all the injured from First and Second World Wars that are facing loneliness, pain, and anger."

"Yes, there are just wars being fought. Look at World War II— that was a just war. Hitler would be ruling over the whole world by now. But please, let's go home. You are a free man. You have done your duty to your country and making a new beginning. Stop talking war, go home and study. I should never have discussed war with you, George. Please don't discuss war with me, I am the wrong person."

"OK, Vivian, you are right. I have a test in German and should look at the words that I need to understand."

"That's what we should have discussed. It would have been fun," she said. "Talk to me in German, George. Let me hear what you can say," she enticed me with a big smile.

"You know, Vivian, right now, I would not know anything. But watch out, next time I know a poem that I have to memorize and I will say it to you."

"Sounds great! I look forward to that."

"About Bill, Vivian, can I go and sit with him or do something?"

"Just ask who is working with Bill, and they will let you know when the times are right. OK, now go home and study. I need to go home to sleep. Good night, dear."

"Thanks, Vivian. See you."

CHAPTER 21

*M*y plant greeted me, I like the lush green leaves with the bright yellow color combination. *Gosh, I had not been home all day.* I felt tired and hungry. I found my unopened books still in my knapsack. I peeled an apple and looked at the poem, not interested in studying. I remember the teacher saying, "You need to know these words. Otherwise, it is hard to remember and discuss the meaning of this very nice poem."

Gee, there are a lot of nouns that I have to look up.

Totally engulfed in my thoughts, I did not hear Ms. Blue Eye call. "Where were you all day, George?"

"Shopping," I said, "and now I am studying my German."

"Will you come to church this weekend? Grandma is asking."

"Yes, if someone picks me up."

Click, and she was gone, just like always. *Gosh, where was I?* She got me out of the study rhythm, so I settled into my red chair with my vocabulary and pencil knowing it was a mistake, but I excused my lack of discipline, hoping I made some headway. *The rest I'll do tomorrow.* And so the weekends come and go.

It was always fun to spend time on the farm and see Angela. We usually talked about school. I helped her wash the dishes. There is another concert coming up around Christmas.

"How about it, George, do you want to come with us?

"Are you going to sing again, Angela?"

"I am not sure. School is heavy at the moment. By the way, we could use some more men in the choir. Why don't you come and see what we are all about?"

"Don't be silly, I cannot sing," I rushed to say.

"That is not what your mom told me. Think about it. I can take you."

"OK, but don't push me. I have enough to do to stay on top of all my present duties. By the way there is a new guy at the center. His name is Bill. His skin is burned badly and really having a lot of troubles. I want to go see him when I have time."

"Yes, I heard about him. Bill is determined to kill himself, I was told. Just like you used to behave. Did you see him yet, George?"

"Yes. I cannot get him out of my mind."

"Yes," Angela said, "I understand George."

"You know, I think you need to stay away from him. This could make you feel depressed again and hinder your grades. They have given that unit two more nurses so that Bill stays safe to gets back on his feet. I hear his behaviour is very hostile with especially female nurses. I hope I will not be assigned to him."

"Why not?"

"I don't think that I could cope with hostility," she said.

Looking at her from the side, I was about to say "You coped with mine," but I held my breath.

Ms. Molly came with a basket full of wrapped-up goodies. "This is for my boy. Take that home. It will keep you from being hungry."

After hugging and thanking her, she said, "I am going to bed. Good night, you two."

"Man, is it that late already? I meant to study my German."

"OK then, but I think you should consider my advice about trying to help Bill," Angela reiterated, then grabbed a sweater, and said, "I am ready to take you home, George. By the way, you need to speak German with me from now on."

"It is too soon, Angela. I need more time. I don't want to make a fool out of myself."

I watched her driving and thought of getting my own car. Angela then said something in German that I did not understand. She went on explaining and repeating the words.

"For Pete's sake, Angela. I am tired, please give me a break."

"I think it's going to be fun, George," she said teasingly, kissing me good night on the cheek. She was watching me get out of the car with her dancing eyes.

I am getting to show you, lady Angela. Give me time, I thought, walking to my apartment. Knowing when she got something in her head, it was stuck and I would have a fight on my hand. I was afraid that communicating with this woman would become difficult from now on, it will be nothing but looking up words in the dictionary.

I wondered about the reason for my pain. *I walked in the fields on uneven ground during the afternoon*, I thought. *Perhaps that might be the culprit.*

I sorted the food into the fridge and the freezer and wondered how I could repay Grandma. It saved me so much time, not having to cook or shop. *I will discuss it with Angela. How the heck would I do that in German?*

It had been a challenging week being on my own, contemplating about Mom and home. I had not called her that weekend. And again, it was the wrong time of day; all were sleeping by now. My red chair looked so good to me, but I sat at the kitchen table to study. I studied a little, just wanted see what the poem sounded like.

I read, "Kuche, Tisch, smecken. Herzen, dankbar, Mutter." I knew the translation of these German words. I made sentences that I could say to Ms. Molly and surprise Angela. I was not tired anymore, so I translated this poem until I understood it pretty well. As I read it aloud, it sounded like someone who was grateful to come home to eat with the family. There was *mother, heart, cake, table,* and *taste it*. These were some words, and it sounded like a celebration. It was eleven thirty. As I was undressing, I felt thankful and remembered *dankbar*, a word in the poem. *I am ready for school tomorrow.*

The days passed quickly, until it was Saturday at 9:00 a.m., when I met my therapist Jim and Dr. Philips. The small talk led to me reporting what I felt physically and mentally; both watched my movements. It made me feel good that Jim seemed very satisfied; Dr. Philips had no comment on my progress. To my big surprise, Dr. Kopp showed up and shook my hand heartily; he seemed to be in great spirits as usually.

"I knew where to find you," he said. "Tell me, do you love your life yet?"

I just smiled at him, unable to find the right words for this great man. I listened to some small talk until Dr. Philips and Jim said their goodbyes and I had to tell my story of the week.

He listened carefully and ended up by saying, "Yes, it's usually the woman that buys flowers. Are you enjoying them, George?"

I motioned. "Yes, I do. How do you have time for me, Dr. Kopp? Aren't you busy today?"

"I have a few minutes before surgery. I knew of the meeting with Jim and Dr. Philips and thought of dropping in. You look great, George."

After a while, he sat forward in his chair, with elbows on his knees, and grabbed my hands. Slowly, he reminded me of how important I was to him and the world.

"You see," he continued, explaining, "the hope that you're spreading by your progress."

I could see nothing but love in his eyes. I held still and listened to his words even though I felt I did not deserve them. He mentioned the people who work there, the vets who are going through difficult times.

"You are still a new story, George. So many of our clients leave after the initial stage of help. They move to other facilities closer to home, and then we do not hear from them. By the way, did you read the story about you in our weekender?"

"What weekender?"

"This is the newspaper of this establishment that is sold on weekends. Lots of people want to know what we do with the money given to us."

"But, Dr. Kopp, I thought that was from the government."

"True, but you have no idea, George, what goes on in this town. The volunteers from all over who work hard on helping individuals like soldiers who have no family or whose family is too far away. Gift giving is a big business, and these folks are a great influence on lonely soldiers and a great help by just being friendly to outsiders.

"For instance, most everybody speaks your language because the town's people know it is the universal language. They hoped that would make communication easy for all concerned. So we keep an eye on guys like you that wanted to kill himself and all people around him, yet you made such a great turnaround. There you have it in a nutshell, George. You look great. I hear you like where you live, and a Ms. Blue Eye is keeping an eye on you."

With a twinkle in his eyes, he stood up, stretching his body and walked to the door. Turning around, he called, "Keep those grades up. That's very important."

I stood there, again feeling I was being told to keep my grades up. *What if I did not? Is that what life is all about? Always being pushed to do more or else? One moment I was a hero and the next a kid.*

I wondered with whom I could talk about the discomfort that I felt at the moment. *Should I visit with Bill?*

Being already at the hospital, I walked toward his room. I heard his screams and nasty words as I got closer. I heard men's voices trying to calm him, and I thought I better leave. *Did I behave like that? How embarrassing that must have been for my mother.*

Looking at the time, I could call now and they would all be home. *Busy signal.*

Just a minute later, my phone rang, and Mom said, "Hi, honey."

"Hi, Mom, so good to hear your voice."

I remember hearing that phrase, "hi, honey," when I had just woken up in the hospital, and I felt the same feelings at this moment. I did not know at that time that I had lost my legs and thought I was home. I told Mom all the news and that I had a conversation with Dr. Kopp that morning and that I was in the newspaper.

Mom's voice was very excited as she said how proud she was of me, her hero.

"I love you, Mom. I am so sorry for the embarrassment I caused you."

I heard Peter shouting, "When are you coming home, George?"

"Not for a while," I said, and then I listened to my eldest brother who had taken the phone from Mom.

"Gosh, it's been so long, David, since I ran away from you bossing me around," I said, and he laughed into the phone.

"It is so good to hear your voice."

"Same here," he said.

I told him of my plan to come for a visit after my first semester, if my money does not run out.

"Don't worry about money, George. You just make that a plan, and we'll take care of it. We are doing well at the moment. The crops are good, and we had the good fortune of having healthy calves. We got a good price for them in the fall.

"George, we had to put down Ella. She was just so old and laid around in the barn for a week without getting up. I took the backhoe and made a ten-foot-deep hole down in the valley by the apple orchard."

After a little while, he said, "She was a good horse."

"The best," I said.

"Yes, we all loved her, and we gave her the best burial a horse could receive. By the way, can you Skype on your computer? I want to show you our new tractor. It's a beauty, George. Find out and we can Skype on Sundays. That way, we can stay better in touch. Here is Mom again."

"I forgot to ask you, George, do you eat enough, being on your own and all?"

I told her how lucky I was knowing Grandma Molly, that I go to church on Sundays with her, and that she sends me home with food lasting until the middle of the week.

She asked whether I see Angela sometimes. I told her that she was bossing me around just like my sister, Margaret.

"Remember when we were little, Mom? That is what Angela is like."

"But she is a lovely young woman and was helpful to you," Mom reminded me.

"She still is, Mom. I see her every Sunday."

"That is good. I am relieved that you hang out with good folks, son, keep it that way. Tell us if you are in need anything. A picture from you would be nice."

"OK, I'll see what I can do about that, Mom."

"What are you going to do this evening, George?"

"I am going to sit in my nice red chair and think of all the good things happening to me, Mom."

"Good, that is good, son. I love you. Don't forget where it all is coming from."

"I knew you were going to say that, Mom. I love you too. I will call you next weekend."

"George, don't forget to say hello to Molly and Angela."

"I won't. Bye for now."

I was hungry and fixed a sandwich to eat with a glass of milk. It had been a busy morning for sure, and I felt satisfied with it all. I figured I really was a lucky fellow to know such good people.

I remembered the newspaper and wondered what it said about me. *Was I really that important? No, George, you are not important. The paper is supposed to tell of how important it is to love one another and how it can heal any ailment we humans suffer from. No doubt about it, I was one lucky guy that had all the love and support one can experience since I returned from duty. Yes, I lost my legs. However, the rest of my body is in working condition. Yes, I am lucky—my mom loving and hovering over me and the doctors and nurses were all helpful and patient while I behaved like a child.*

Oh God, be with my friends in the fields and maybe with Bill, who is fighting all the demons that control his will at this time. When will he understand that the people around him want the best for him? It took a long time for me, in spite of Mother at my bedside. Not having a family must be difficult for Bill.

I wondered what reason he had to sign up. Those recruiters are trained to highlight the military just to sign you up. Bill, not having family, probably thought that going into the army might be the best for him. Who knows what his motivation was to sign his name under these famous words—"I will bear faith and allegiance to the flag." I thought, if I befriend myself a little and make an effort to get to know Bill, he might lose some of his hostility.

CHAPTER 22

*I*t was Sunday on the farm after church with the family. I liked listening to the guys argue, even though I did not understand, but it reminded me of home. We were a loud bunch too. Someone realized that the guest did not understand, and they all switched over to English, amazing.

"Did you ever help build a house, George?" Greg asked.

"No, not lately," I said.

"Well, we are thinking of doing it ourselves. It is very hard to get people nowadays, with all the construction going on. The brick-layers make good money working for big companies, and nobody wants to be a laborer anymore."

"With winter not being far out, you need to get going soon," I contributed, remembering it being said that homes built in winters often have something wrong with them.

"Your winters are much colder than ours here in Germany. You see, sometimes we don't even wear winter clothes."

"Well, I will find out soon enough," I said and wondered if I could walk to school in the winter.

"Want another beer before dinner, George?"

"I better not," I heard myself say, even though I wanted to drink another. *I must buy a case of beer for next time*, I thought while they were talking.

I watched Angela going from kitchen to dining room being teased by her brothers. *She was giving them back well*, I thought. It was all done with affection, being the only girl. *Oh yes, family is the best establishment in the world*, I thought. Again, my thoughts drifted to Bill and that scarred face. *He sure has an uphill future without folks supporting him.*

"Move over," Angela's mother said. "What are you thinking about, sitting here so quiet by yourself?"

"I don't feel like I am alone. I was just thinking of how lucky I am to be treated as though I am family. You know, Barbara, I feel like I almost belong. Thank you so much for having me."

"You looked pretty worried there for a minute," she said, patting my arm.

I continued with my thoughts. "Well, you caught me thinking of Bill, a buddy at the hospital that is not doing well."

"Is that the burnt soldier, George?"

"Yes. How do you know him Barbara?"

"I passed a young volunteer running down the hall the other day crying. I asked her what was wrong. Judy, the nurse trying to keep up with her, told me later of how rotten he treated this volunteer. Apparently, this Bill must have a rough history from what is being said, but don't take my word for it."

"I feel sorry for him. If you see his face, you can't help wonder how these doctors are able to do something with it," I said. "He is supposed to go for the third surgery this coming week. I know he has no family. Don't get me wrong, Barbara, I don't excuse his ill manners by any means. I am told that I behaved poorly when I came here. How embarrassing it must have been for my mom."

"You are right, George. I remember your mom walking the halls with her head to the floor, not to show her teary eyes."

Shaking my head in utter disgust, I said, "My poor mom." I looked around thinking of Bill, wondering if he ever felt secured as I did at that moment with people just sitting and having a beer on a Sunday with a family. *Bill probably has not experienced this kindness,* I thought.

"We just don't know Bill as yet, but maybe we can help him to feel love," I mentioned.

Barb got up, and Ms. Molly took the seat, bringing her arm under mine, grinning.

"How is my boy?"

"I am good, Ms. Molly," I said.

"Tell me, do you have a microwave in your apartment?"

"Yes, I do."

"That is good," she said. She leaned back and just sat with me.

"I thought I noticed a flash. Did you see that flash?" I asked, turning to the old lady.

"I did not," she said.

It was like a camera flash, I wondered.

"Look at this!" Joe shouted. "If that isn't the best picture you have ever seen."

"Leave them alone." Angela walked over to call them in for dinner.

"Grandma has a new boyfriend."

"Right you are," she said as she got up, patting my arm. "Let's eat, son."

I had some trouble getting off the couch. Angela held her hand out and pulled me up.

"That's embarrassing," I said, "but the couch is so low and soft."

"Come, sit here. This is a good chair," she said.

I was wondering what the difference was; all the chairs looked alike.

As usual, everybody wanted to put food on my plate. It happened every time I ate with them.

"Do I look that hungry?"

"We just want to make sure you don't go home hungry," Barb said.

"Everyone in our house fills their own plate," I said.

"Don't worry. We do that in our house," Angela said, moving an empty bowl and replaced it with a full one.

"How do you like the potato salad I made, George?"

"It is the only thing she can cook," Joe said.

"Hush," Ms. Molly said, "Angela is getting pretty good at cooking a meal. Any man taking her for a wife will not go hungry. Here try it, George."

I felt uneasy, though I did not know why.

"What is all that green stuff in here, Angela? I thought this was a potato salad, not a mixture of kitchen leftover," Joe continued, teasing.

"Mr. Know-It-All, these are radishes, green onion, parsley, and the last of the piece I picked this morning. Nothing old about this salad. Anything else you want to complain about?"

I had great difficulty trying not to laugh. Angela's face—as a matter of fact, her whole body—straightened up, ready to give that little twit as she called her brother a good fight, even though he was several inches taller than Angela.

Joe looked at me and burst out laughing, saying, "It's all right, George. I just wanted you to see how beautiful my sister is when she gets mad."

"You better watch it, George," she said. "Don't let me go there."

"Go where, Angela? I did not do a thing. I was just looking at you, and I must say your brother is definitely right. You are very pretty when you're angry."

"Kibitzing is just one of those things that happen at dinners with big families," said Barb. "As long as it is seasoned with love."

"Well," said Ms. Molly, "I feel the spirit is with us." With that, she finished the discussion.

After dessert, I helped bring dishes to the kitchen but soon found out I was hindering the three women so I walked out and sat with the men.

Joe came with another beer, sitting beside me. "Tell me, brother hero, where do you think the war is going? Do you believe we will end up winning?"

"No, Joe. There is no winner in this fight. I think we have been told stories by President Bush about weapons of mass destruction. We have been hearing about the Axis of Evil so much that we came to believe it. Iraq is devastated, and the USA is making a lot of enemies. Iraqi people will hate us forever. We will be there long after the war has ended, trying to clean up the mess we created."

"How do you know, George?"

"I do not know, but I hear so much from soldiers coming in to the center having left parts of their body in the dust or have burns on their body, being a daily memory of where they were. These dubious allegations that Saddam Hussein is a threat to the Western world is nonsense."

"A terrible loss for so many," Joe said. "I am glad Germany stayed out of it this time."

I did not feel like talking war and was glad when Angela was ready to drive me home. I hoped she would show me how Skype worked on the computer. She noticed the flowers still looking good and mentioned that I did not neglected them.

"Lucky me, I gave it some water before I went to church," I said.

"You have the application on your computer. Here, I'll show you, but you have to call home and see when they have time to talk with you because they have to open to Skype also. So let's do that." Angela looked at the clock. "It's nighttime in the US now."

"Darn, next week, we will make sure. Maybe Saturday is a good day."

"Makes sense," Angela agreed. "I will come at noon. We can go for lunch or something after we talk to your family."

Suddenly, she switched to German, asking if I was tired. Of course, I did not know what she said.

"Well, you know the first two words," she said, folding her hands together, bending her head and closing her eyes, laying her head.

"Are you asking if I am tired?"

"So, tell me in German."

I knew the word *mude* was "tired."

I showed her the poem I was learning to say in German.

"So read it to me."

"OK, don't laugh," I said.

"Why not? It is my turn to laugh at you. Ha-ha."

She listened attentively.

"Great," she said, "You read very well. What else can you say?"

I showed her my notes and read sentences to her.

"Wow that is great. All these phrases you can use daily, do you, George?"

"No, I am scared people don't understand me."

137

"But if you don't use them, you will not find out if you are not being understood. You speak clear enough for me that I know what you are saying. We started to use the English language just like that with phrases and had fun laughing at one another.

"Do you like your teacher, George? Ursula?"

"She is all right," I said.

"In German, please."

No problem, I thought. *It's a yes or no question. I could do that without looking at my notebook.*

"You like her that much?" Angela quipped. "Now, tell me if she is pretty in German."

"Let me see."

Angela was holding my notes close to her body.

"Without notes," She said.

What to say? Careful, George. So I said *nein*—meaning, "no."

"Next question. Is she old or young? In German, bitte."

I said yes.

"Yes what? Old or young, George?"

"Alt," I said.

It seemed to satisfy her.

"That's enough for today, Angela. I am tired."

"Me too. OK, George. I will see you next Saturday. Have a good week. Good night. Wait, I have the food grandma sent for you in the car."

"Angela, I need to ask you. How can I repay what your grandma does for me? I want to pay her or somehow show my appreciation."

"She would not take your money, I know that for sure, George. You know, she just wants to be good to you, knowing that you are so far from home. I will think about it and let you know." she said as she walked to her car.

She tiptoed and kissed me good night, and I thanked her for the day.

Suddenly, I thought of something. *What is it? Let me see.* I looked at the dashboard of her car to see how much gas she had.

Puzzled, she said, "What?"

"Nothing," I said, and she was gone.

That's what I will do, I thought. *I will fill her tank with gas when she needs it. I will repay Angela at least for all the driving.*

Months flew by—September, October, and November. It had turned cold but not really cold like at home but still cold. We had snow in Oklahoma for two weeks; I watched the white stuff coming down on Skype. What a great application. I talked with my family just like I was sitting with them at home.

Peter wanted to know when I was coming home for Christmas. I told him that I am not sure, that I have got to think about it.

How quickly one can make a mistake, I thought, taking a pop out of the cooler. I had not given it any thought; I was busy and happy and really did not want to miss visiting Bill, even though he could be a real heel.

At times he would ask, "Why do you come here anyway?"

I would tell him that I hoped being his friend might help a little.

His face would change into an ugly, belittling grin and call me dumb shit or something even worse. I usually just walked away from him, feeling hurt. I wondered often what kind of guy he was before he got burned in the field. *What kind of a kid had he been? Did he have a home? He must have had at one time. Was he abused or did he see a lot of it where he lived?* I just could not imagine anybody behaving so rotten as though he enjoyed giving pain to others.

I knew roughnecks at home when we were kids, but it was never meant to give pain as I recalled. Oh man, those were good days, riding our bikes, showing off the stunts we had developed. Haymaking was extra fun. Neighbors came together and helped each other because times were short for haymaking. We fooled around a lot growing up. It saddened me a little thinking if I had not left home. *I better stop right there.*

Actually, Bill had never asked who I was or what I was doing. I told him that I am in school and could not come any oftener. It did not seem to interest him. He was in his own world, "a hellhole" as he called it. Still, I wanted to give him a little more time to see if I was really helping him.

Maybe after his face healed, he could tolerate himself better. But no, Bill was not a good excuse for not flying home during my vacation. Yes, the other thing is, I wanted to have a good paycheck and not feel dependent on the government check.

"I am doing OK. I don't need to go home," I confirmed to myself. What was keeping me from wanting to see my family? "The truth is, George, you don't want to open that door because you really feel very uneasy and downright ashamed meeting family and friends that had become successful individuals and productive while you had become an invalid, dependent on a government check."

Another thing is, I would have to sleep in the same room as my little brother. He would see my leg stumps—how embarrassing. All these things bothered me.

"I am different, I am not the same George," I lamented, talking to myself.

Had I given up my identity too? Why did I feel so detached from my folks? I could no help it, but suddenly I felt very emotional.

After a while, I thought of talking with someone about my feelings, and who else but my mom would be that person? Mother saw me at my worst.

Home, I must go home, it mattered. You must go home, George, don't be a loner. Take your feelings to your kin. They could probably help discover some things about yourself. That person would be Mother. It was Mom that tolerated me. She suffered all this grief, sadness, and tears. She should know my struggles of trying to become a whole man again. It made sense.

CHAPTER 23

I walked to the chapel. It was a good way to end the day. Maybe I would meet a buddy at the center. It was good sitting there alone, and as usual the emptiness and the quiet made me feel excepted—even empty. Empty of what? I could not explain it, but I enjoyed sitting there.

I sat alone until I felt the squeezing of hands on my shoulders.

"Father Paul, what the heck?"

"Good to see you here," he said. "Are you keeping out of trouble?"

"As far as I know. Maybe if I had more time, I might like to get into trouble just a little," I said.

Shaking my hand, he said, "I heard you made it into the paper?"

"Just keeping busy," I said. "So what brings you here on a quiet Sunday, Father Paul?"

"Not so quiet, George, lots to pray about."

"I did not hear the chopper," I said, raising my voice. My sense of peace left me, thinking, *What did I miss? Did new buddies arrive? I should have been there.*

"Don't, don't get all wound up. Everything is in control."

Amazing. My thighs started to jerk. I put my hand on both thighs, and it stopped.

A phone rang, and Father Paul got up, answering his cell, and left.

I left the chapel and walked toward Bill's room, wondering how he might feel. My inner peace left me, and like a cold shower, I was filled with guilt for neglecting my buddies.

Bill's room was empty—bed stripped, just the black mattress staring at me. All his paraphernalia like creams, the special water glass, and the magazines were gone, except for that strange odor, which I still noticed and even heavier than usual.

They moved him, I thought.

I felt dazed and walked to the hall, hoping to find someone to talk with. There was no one I knew, but I got a soft drink out of the cooler and sat at a table alone, brooding. I heard loud voices from some corner.

Bill, what happen to you? I wondered. *Whatever it is, Father God, be with him.* I actually was amazed that I was saying these words, but they felt good.

It was too early to go home, and so I marched to see Jess for a spell.

"Man, you look like you need a beer, George. What is happening in your life? Sit down. Have one on me," he said, walking to the kitchen for a can of beer.

"No thanks. Not tonight, Jess."

So we sat.

"You feel like talking," he remarked, bumping his elbow against my ribs.

"I don't know. It's nothing, except Bill. Maybe you've heard of him, the burned guy? He was not in his room, and his bed is stripped. Wonder what happened to him."

I got no answer for a while, and then Jess said, "Yes, I got to know him pretty well. I didn't know you got acquainted, George. A very sad case, I tell you. So that is what is bothering you? He got transferred all the way home to Texas to a special burn unit that is better equipped than Landstuhl."

"Why didn't they do that in the first place? And better equipped? That is hard to believe," I said.

"Because there was so much else wrong with him. That needed to stabilize him. I heard that Bill doesn't want to get better, a strange individual and very difficult to satisfy. There is no medication strong enough to keep him out of trouble. I've been told he was on dope before he went in the army, and paramedics found him doped up in combat, apparently burned to bits from his own mistake."

"I think I'll have that beer now, Jess," I said. "That is a lot to digest. I am grateful for your company, Jess."

"You know, George. When you have been burned and went through hell for a long time with surgeries and isolation, one wonders frequently, is life worth so much pain? We all changed after fighting that war."

"How do you know?" I looked at Jess from the side, and then our eyes met for a long, steady while.

"I know, George, I know."

I watched him as he rolled up his right arm, and with his left hand, he pointed to the right side of his body down to his leg.

"All of that was at, one time, raw flesh, George. There are no words of what the individual goes through. I tell you, I wanted to die many times when they took me to the cleaning area three times a week. I had no control over what was done for me. I was placed into this warm water bath that was not so bad, but when the nurses tried to take the sloughed-off skin, sometimes they had to cut it off, George. It was unbearable.

"I was in and out of shock frequently. The pain medication made me restless, and I pulled out intravenous from my left hand and arm that provided me with fluids like blood, plasma, and water to prevent dehydrations and total organ failure. The bed needed changing two and three times daily because I was oozing constantly through my wounds. I tell you, George, the nurses had to change their clothing each time coming in my room. They were angels. I had no control of what was decided for my body.

"Never, never I heard a negative word out of them. Matter of fact, they cried with me, and laughed with me, telling jokes to help me. My chances of dying were much better than living for a long, long time. The battle with infection was constant. Apparently, the burns on my right thigh were so deep that to prevent blood infection, they were thinking of amputating my leg, totally in the hands of doctors and nurses."

Aghast, I looked at him. I didn't know my eyes were watering.

"It's OK, friend"—he hit my side with his elbow—"I should not have told you all this."

"Look at me now, George, here I am making a living—a *new life*—I have a new life, George. Emma is good to me and tries to understand when I feel moody and want to be alone. I am not so sure of her family being ready to accept an invalid coming into their life. But I tell you, anybody coming home from that war is marked for life, mentally and physically. There is not a day that I am not reminded of having been burned. When the sun is hot and I am out too long or even behind in the kitchen, I feel my new skin stretching. When it rains, I feel my leg pains me, but that's life."

A family with two boys came in, and Jess walked to the counter to serve them. I watched him as he patted the children's head, shouting, "What will it be, folks?" smiling at them.

His attractive smile was like a magnet; you feel like talking, not just ordering what you wanted. This family did not know anything about what Jess had gone through. Did he have pain at this moment? The children licked their ice cream, walking by me.

Jess shouted, "Let's have another beer and go home, George."

"Not for me, Jess, but I will sit with you. Will it ever end, Jess?"

"Well, I tell you there's a lot of action going on. Mostly women are very much against this war. I just read about the march on the white House. Books have been written, like *Iraq*, Vets against the War, Veterans for Peace, Mothers against the Draft, but I don't know if anything will come out of it. Here in Germany it's quiet. I hear very little about war. Remember the Germans had their share."

"What do people say here in Germany? Do you hear them talk about war at all?"

"Well, we cannot compare with the USA because Germany, as a whole, is anti any war since WWII. And if they talked war, it won't be around Americans. I feel there is still a lot of shame of what they did during WWII to the Jews."

"I like it here, Jess. The people are so friendly and helpful, wherever I meet them."

"Don't forget, George, the USA was very good to Germany after they bombed the heck out of every town. Also, I realize Germany paid every penny back owed to the US. Look how this town is prospering from the building alone of this hospital center. It is like a city in itself. As I see it, that was not built in the interest of Germany.

"George, remember we needed a hospital big enough to combine all the others in various towns for the heavy casualties coming from the fields and they were our men and women in need of immediate care? To fly them to the USA was too far. Most wounded would have succumbed. The very best doctors from all over the world concentrate here to work. They like the cleanliness and the peaceful lifestyle and stay. Have you been around much yet, George?"

"I've just been to the market on the weekend and loved the atmosphere of sitting around and having coffee on sidewalks. I had not seen that at home."

"We have museums, concert halls, magnificent architecture built by German and American engineers working in harmony. All of this can be done in peacetime, George."

"Yes, Jess. But we had to get rid of Hitler first, remember? That was a necessary war, if there ever was one. I read some history about that long and bloody fight."

"Yes, it took so many men in uniform, not to mention all the civilians. Let's lock up, George." He walked behind the counter, cleaning up and counting his cash.

"OK, I am done, George, let's go. I am going home too."

"See you around. Good night, Jess, thanks for the beer."

My open notebook invited me when I got home. I started to read and found comfort in my studies. My counsellor was satisfied in most all subjects, but she mentioned that I needed to bring up my grades in anatomy, if I wanted to get financial help.

It was a fascinating class, but it had so much memorizing. I remember Ms. Munroe telling me that it will get better. I wondered what she meant by that. I had learned about body structure, about the function of the body, very interesting cell functions and the many individual cells for each organ of the body has its own life and activity. Each day I appreciated the marvels of our body more and wondered if we would learn about it during our young school days society as a whole would treat our bodies better. No, but I appreciated to the fullest the daily opportunities I had learning and becoming the best, a useful individual. I loved my life at this minute.

Well, another month, I thought, *and then I begin the second half of the first year.* I realized it was still a long time before I will make a living.

Maybe going home would be a good idea, sharing my good fortune with family and friends at home would be a good idea.

When all my
means have
reached the end
then His is just
beginning.

CHAPTER 24

*C*hristmas business started in November, and it reminded me of being home. *Should I, should I not? I had enough money, though, but not much left over for gifts, but I would make Mom happy. My grades were very good, and I will receive the needed stipend from the government for my grades. Of course, that was borrowed money.*

I felt glad going home after the last class for that day. Sitting in my favourite chair, opening a letter from big brother David, I found a ticket from Lufthansa to fly on December 18 direct to Oklahoma. I looked at the piece of paper, turned it, and noticed how precisely my brother got the time of my of school correct; I could not believe it. I wondered if Angela had something to do with it.

No, David does not know her that well. Aha! But my mother does.

Instead of feeling grateful, I felt an immediate anger. "David is still telling me what to do. Brother, I am a man and don't need your help, you son of a gun, you have been telling me what to do all my life. I am not your little brother anymore. Thank you, but no thanks for the ticket. I must make an end to his behaviour right now."

Again, I realized the time difference. *They are sleeping, so there is no use calling now. But I will tell him*, I thought.

Flying out on that date would only give me a week to get ready. Jumping up, I felt some pain behind my right knee. *That is all I need*, I thought.

Maybe I will see Angela and discuss things with her. She finished her classes the same time I did. She is probably out doing some Christmas shopping. Why am I so anxious? Everything seems to be happening right now. Looking out the window, there was no snow as yet.

Apache usually had snow at this time of year. Even as small as my village is, at Christmastime, folks went all out with decorating. Loudspeakers played Christmas music without stopping. Many trees were decorated, and church bells chimed hourly. I liked this time of the year. Gifts were piling up in the living room. When we were kids, we were not supposed to go into the living room; nevertheless, we'd sneak and look at the names on the pretty packages whenever there was a chance.

Home, I had a good home, and I considered how lucky I was, seeing the turmoil in other areas of the world. This was only my third Christmas away from home. What about my buddies who were away longer and continued fighting, destroying other people's homes? What a crazy world we live in. I wondered what Ann was doing with her baby boy around this time without her husband. What about all the people at the veteran's hospitals around the world? All have a story to tell, men sitting possibly alone. Maybe I should stay and keep company with the ones who are alone in the center.

I will look around tomorrow, I thought. And with that, I got ready for bed, hoping I could get rid of my mixed-up feelings.

I dialed Angela the next morning.

"Oh, I was just going to call you, George. What's up?"

"Well, I am all confused, Angela. Do you have time to listen to me?"

"Goodness, what is the matter, George? What happened?"

"No, no, it's nothing bad. My folks sent me a ticket to fly home."

"How great is that, George? When are you going?"

"I don't know if I am going. I wanted to buy my own ticket if I were going."

"What for? Just give them the money back when you make a salary, if you don't want to accept the gift."

"That is a good idea, Angela. Dear, what would I do without you?"

"Say that in German."

"Not now, Angela. Will you help me get some gifts? I couldn't believe how quickly I had made up my mind taking your idea going home. The ticket is for the eighteenth."

"That is soon. Sure, my favourite thing to do spending some-one else's money. Soon, we both will be off the hook, George. No school. Let's have some fun shopping. I will meet you in an hour. And we'll make a list."

I better get my legs on, shave, and make my bed, I thought.

As usual Angela arrived on time, smiling into the morning.

"I like that sweatshirt you are wearing, Angela. Great colour on you. Where did you get it?"

"It's my mother's. I don't know where she bought it. So, what is on the agenda for you, what do you want to do?"

"Angela, I need to buy some gifts for my family, and I don't know where to begin."

"Let's make a list, George."

"How is that supposed to help me? I know the names of my folks, but I just have no idea what they want. I have not seen them for so long. Last time I saw my brother Peter, he needed new tires for his bike."

"Let's ask your mother."

"Well, that is of no use. She is going to tell me not to buy any-thing, just come home."

"Do you want me to talk with her?"

"If you want to, here, I will call her. It is afternoon at home."

"Good timing let's."

"Hello, who? Oh, Angela from Germany?"

"No, no, he is standing right beside me. Sorry I frightened you. He is so elated coming home and needed to know what to buy for Christmas. No, school will finish in a few weeks."

Man, oh man. When women get together, is this never ending? I thought.

They haven't even started shopping for Christmas. I poured myself some coffee. How old I heard eight-month-old Monika had become. That is easy. I love to shop for Jessica, watching her enthu-siasm growing by leaps and bounds.

"OK. Here he is. It's your mom, George. Talk with her. Don't be too long. We have things to do."

151

As I listened to Mother, I was amazed. She sounded different than before. Her voice sounded authoritative, like I was that boy at home.

"Listen to Angela," she said.

What is going on? I thought, but I had no time to ponder the question because Angela was tarring on my new shirt.

"I want to see what you wrote, Angela, before we spend money."

"George, do you have a picture of baby Jessica"

"Someplace around here. What do you want with it?"

"I wonder if she looks like her mom. It's OK, don't spend time looking for it now. How much money do you have, George?"

"I have a couple hundred. That's all."

"Mm, that's enough for today."

As we drove into town, I was hoping that we would not spent all of my two hundred dollars.

"I have not been in this part of town. It is very busy here, Angela."

"It's Saturday, George, and Christmas."

"Last minutes to shop before Christmas—*Weinachten*, in German."

What a nice word. It sounds musical," she said. "And that is what's on the minds of folks now."

"Let's talk German today."

"Angela, please do not push me."

"Oh, Georgy boy, you are moody. What do you want?" She kissed me on the cheek and smiled.

"I don't really know what I want, but nothing feels right."

"We have been sitting here in this parked car, wasting time. Let's go walk down the street. George, you will get in mood for Weinachten," she said, giving me a gentle push toward the door.

After a while, I felt better. It felt so natural having Angela by my side as we passed the windows with our reflections. She was babbling about a picture frame for my sister and her husband.

I remembered that he was flying a chopper. I still didn't know where he was. *I hope he gets home to raise his daughter*, I thought.

"What do you think, George? I believe that will be a nice gift. Let's go in."

So it went all morning, being dragged here, there, and everywhere. I noticed the shirt Angela was wearing hanging at a nice store, something like Macy's department store in Oklahoma and said, "I want this for my mom. She will like it."

"What color, George?"

"I think the same as yours would look nice on her."

"Let's see if they have the size she needs."

"Have it gift wrapped for her."

"Gift wrapping is too expensive here. I will do all that at home," she said.

It was noon, and we decided on pizza for lunch.

"Try to order in Deutsch for me."

"I will, only if you don't laugh at me, Angela."

She decided on number three.

Not too hard, I thought. *To make it short, I would like the same.*

"Fur mich das selbe, bitte" (The same for me, please).

"You are cheating, my friend." She waved a finger at me. "But wait until you see what you ordered. You will regret ordering something you don't know."

"OK, Angela. Would you share a beer with me?"

"OK, I will."

I am at your mercy as usual, I thought, a feeling I did not like. But I enjoyed the quiet moments while we ate. I thought about the money I had spent on gifts for home and nothing yet for friends. Had to admit, Angela really was a big help, and it went quickly.

"Thank you very much, Angela, for being here with me," I said.

"It's costing you, George." Her dancing eyes were on the dessert menu.

When the waiter came, I pointed to the picture and said in German, "Zwei, bitte."

While Angela was licking her desert, I asked her what her mom and grandmother might like for Christmas.

"Mom likes perfume."

"What about you? Do you like perfume?"

"I love it, but I cannot afford it. Not until I make better money."

Great, I thought.

As we walked through another store to get to our car, we passed a decorated area with all kinds of cosmetics.

Angela pulled on my sweatshirt. "Look, George, I want to watch this for a moment."

So we stood and watched as the client listened to suggestions and trials of different colors for her eyebrows. I looked into Angela's face; she was fascinated with what was going on. I kissed her lightly on her right cheek and whispered in her ear, "Angela, you are so beautiful. You need none of this."

"But I want to watch this, George."

"OK, I am walking around here."

Wandering through the aisles, I thought, *What in the world possessed me to kiss her? The emotion came on so suddenly. I hope Angela does not think anything special about this silly impulse.*

Walking around between the many shoppers, I thought it should be easy to find gifts, looking at all the wonderful packages for men and women. A beautiful young woman invited me to try a cologne for men.

She handed me a little, white card. "Smell it, soldier, and tell me if you like it."

Flustered and a little stunned being called *soldier*, I looked at this person in front of me. She wore a white blouse, showing too much cleavage.

Angela, suddenly beside me, looked at me. "What is going on here, George?"

I handed Angela the card.

"For me?" she said, frowning.

"No, for me. What do you think?"

"We have other things to do. I don't like it," she said, not even looking at the outreached hand of the clerk and pulled me away.

"Angela, wait a minute. Tell me, do I look like a soldier to you?"

"Don't be silly. I know you have been one. No, she should not have called you a soldier. Does that bother you, George?"

It did bother me. She probably thought of it as a compliment.

Walking between aisles, Angela asked, "Are you excited about seeing everybody, George?"

I thought a little and said, "Angela, I am scared. Sometimes I wish I could stay here and hide or be with my buddies that cannot be home to celebrate Christmas."

"Don't do that to yourself, George." She took her hands and shaking my shoulders. "They all will be so happy to see you. I don't understand your fear, or is it a lack of confidences? Are there things at home you don't like to be reminded of?"

I shook my head. "No, no, Angela, it is just that I don't like the fuss my folks will be making over me. We should be making a fuss over the guys that are fighting for their lives every moment. Here I am warm, safe, eating turkey, and having fun. I just don't feel good about all that." Kissing the palm of her hand, I said, "Sorry, dear, I am just a sentimental fool."

"You are a very good person, George, thinking of your buddies. What we can do together for the men and women out there is pray for their safety. But you did your duty and should not feel that you do not have the right to be happy to go home and celebrate the birth of Christ."

"It's only a week away. You realize that, Angela?"

"I will miss you, George. Will you take the time to call me?"

"We will Skype, and you'll see everybody. Let's go, Angela. I get anxious just thinking of what lies ahead next week. I want to fill your car with gas, and I would like you to tell me what to get for your mom and Ms. Molly before we drive home."

Those two ladies were no problem to make happy, and in minutes we bought what I thought would be a nice gift and I did not mind the money spent.

"Let's pick up the paper to wrap everything to take home. Would you like to do that?"

"Why not?" she said.

That afternoon and most of the evening was spent at Angela's house.

Walking in the kitchen, the aroma of vanilla reminded me of home.

Ms. Molly looked at all the stuff we bought, saying, "Looks a lot like Christmas, George. Are you excited yet?"

"Every day is Christmas just looking at you, Ms. Molly," I said.

From behind, I heard Joe shout, "That's about right, George. What would we do without our Oma?"

"Hush all of you!" she shouted back. "Come taste my cookies."

Joe took a plate of warm sweets into the living room. A large evergreen was being worked on.

"Joe, grab me that bundle over there. Hold it while I take these crystals out one by one."

Between beer and jokes, the night came; and I ended up with the spirit of Christmas. *What a day it was*, I thought, falling on top of the bed, thinking of all the things Angela and I had conquered. I spent more money than I had wanted and still had to take care of Angela and maybe get a little something for some of the individuals who helped me stay sane at the center.

Shucks, there were Dr. Kopp and Father Paul, I almost forgot. I will write them a card. That has to do it. I thought about their dedication, always being ready to stretch out to the need of individuals in need. I felt love for both and all the others nurses, Jim, and Dr. Philips.

Might as well get ready for bed, I said to myself, taking of the legs I call the prostheses. Something in my brain gets a trigger, and a hostility like a heartburn breaks out in me. I fight it every night.

Here it comes, I thought. I tried thinking of the fantastic day I had with Angela and her family to overcome this negative emotion. Slowly feeling warm and secure in bed, I thought of my buddies, the man with no arms and legs, Ann without her husband Joe, and John the burned man. I prayed that the Almighty be by their side.

These were my routine thoughts before I found sleep. It begins with taking off the prostheses, looking at my stumps, and realizing how difficult it will be for someone to love and with whom to share a life. *Who wants to look at a man without legs for the rest of their life? There is no room for romance, George. Get it in your head, George. You are a marked man for life. Stop sulking, it is what it is.*

Comparing my lot with all the other men and women coming home from war somehow gave me peace. *In other words, I was not so bad off*, I thought.

CHAPTER 25

I was reading Christmas cards at a variety store as Dr. Philips tapped my shoulders.

"Look at you, George, what a gorgeous hunk of man. Give me a hug. Merry Christmas, dear."

She seemed really happy to see me. On that note, I said, "And I am flying home for the holidays."

"Yes, I will be back before school" answered her immediate question about school.

"That is great. Make sure of coming back and look at you reading Christmas cards in German. You have come a long way, my dear. Frohe Weinachten, George, my regards to your family."

Am I ready to write those in German? I decided to give it a try. I passed a window decked with ladies' lingerie. *Would a guy really go in there and buy something for a girlfriend? Not me*, I thought. *But if that girlfriend became my wife, that would be OK.*

"Do you know the size of your friend?" this voice said. Beside me stood the woman from yesterday who called me "soldier."

I did not turn toward her but looked at her reflection in the window. She was Angela's size but had a smaller frame. *Nice*, I thought.

"Are you coming in?"

Eventually I said OK.

"I'll help you, let's go."

"No thanks, I will come later."

I needed to avoid her because she confused me.

I had a coffee and called Angela.

"I forgot to get a suitcase for my luggage, Angela," I lamented into the phone.

As usual, she had the answer. "Just borrow mine and buy one later when they go on sale, George. Tell you what, I will come over and bring them. We can pack a little, getting you ready for Saturday. Where are you? I'll pick you up."

"I am a few steps from the Pizza Hut."

"OK, give me thirty minutes."

Again, there was nothing I could say, Angela is always in the lead, and I did not like this part of her personality.

I walked a few steps, looking into shops. I saw a woman holding up a sweater in front of herself; it was Angela's blue color. I watched her turning it upside down and inside out, saying, "Wunderbar" (Beautiful).

I did not need much time to think. I wanted it for Angela; it was the perfect gift. The elderly saleswoman asked me for a size, and I told her the one that the lady before me had handled would probably be the right size.

"You can return it if it is too large," the clerk said as she folded it. "The Scottish cashmere was the best one could buy." She showed various colors of wrapping paper, and I chose red with a white ribbon. It looked beautiful.

"Two hundred Euros, please."

I felt like I was hit with a hammer. Blushingly, I paid the lady and walked out penniless. *George, you have lots to learn. Why not say it was too expensive? Why not ask before you purchased?*

Well, I had to learn not to be hasty, remembering how quickly I had signed my contract to get in the army. It was only money, and it was for my best friend; even so, she annoyed me making decisions for me.

Of course, the first question upon seeing the lovely packaging Angela asked was, "Who is that for? Did you buy it here?" She almost shouted, "This is the most expensive store in town. I hope you know what you are doing, George."

"I was going to buy pizza for lunch, but I have no money left."

"Serves you right," she spouted out.

"Can we go to the bank and see how much I have left? I need some pocket money for when I head home."

I was in luck because Christmas day fell on Thursday this year. The pension checks had come in the bank three days before the normal date.

"Let's have some pizza and a beer," I said, very relieved I had money.

I felt so happy having a precious gift for Angela. *Was I finally done with shopping?*

We ate, and I listened to Angela's ideas about the New Year, working as a "real" nurse, as she kept on calling it. She mentioned that she would like to specialize in psychology after a while, but she said she would wait and see what was offered at the center.

Hopping into Angela's car was surly easier than taking a bus and so much faster, I pondered.

The meeting with my trainer Jim and Dr. Philips was uneventful the next day.

"Stay in touch. Come in anytime. Be a show-off to guys that are just starting up, to give them hope."

Dr. Philips questioned how I was feeling about myself. It was not easy to answer. I had to think about it, but then I told her about my wandering mind every night, beginning by taking off my legs nightly. It was the reminder of war and frequently wondering what my buddies whom I left fighting without me were doing.

"You know, Dr. Philips, I feel downright guilty at times," I said.

She listened attentively but had nothing to say about how to fix those feelings other then telling me that they will fade in time.

Jim excused himself shortly after giving some of his favorite advice, and Dr. Philips's compliments left me with mixed emotion.

Wandering into the empty dining room, two older men in uniform sat by me and were talking about how to get back there.

"Well, lad, how about you, you look fit enough, George?"

Strange, I thought, *he knows my name.*

"Fit enough for what?" I said.

"To sign up and get back into action?"

I don't know what I did, but both men got up, pushing their chair away from under them. One of them said, "Think about it, buddy," and then they walked away.

What made me think they might be recruiters? No, not here in the hospital, would they? Without looking back, they waved their hands and wished me a Merry Christmas.

"We will be back, George."

I was alone for some time, thinking of what just happened. I tried to sort out what I had heard. These guys made me feel uncomfortable.

Walking to the chapel, I sat in my corner, analyzing the pangs in my heart. *"We will be back." Could they recruit me? Here I am sitting high and dry while there was a war going on. These guys were planting a seed in me, that's what it was.*

"But, God, I just came from there. I did my duty. I don't believe that you want us there." My eyes watered, thinking of my best buddy Joe talking about his sweetheart Ann being so cautious of weight gain during pregnancy in her notes to him.

Should I have been more forceful? Should I not have let him go on guard that night? He would be home with his baby and wife.

"My fault. God, was it my fault? Do I need to go back there?" Dazed, I walked to my apartment, not realizing that it snowed until I got home and looked out into the backyard. The ground was white. *Nice, yes, very nice.* It's Christmas, but my soul felt sad for the guys in the field. *Go serve your country, George.*

Coming out of a dream with familiar feelings of dampness yet without the pressure of gear on my body awakened me. I jumped out from my chair on my stumps.

Oh God, my legs! I was shocked for a moment. Seeing the prostheses, I recovered quickly. My watch said it was 1:30 a.m. Wednesday morning. *It was a nasty dream. I haven't had one of those for a long time.*

I drank some water and looked outside; snow was still falling. I fell onto my bed, reevaluating my dream. *No, George, don't go there. Forward, forward.*

I forgot who said these words to me. For sure, that someone had two legs to stand on. *How do I get used to seeing myself standing on stumps? But it is a fact, George.*

"Get with it," I said aloud.

I leaned against the headboard of the bed and covered myself. *I wish I were not alone.*

I picked up the little Bible that my mom had given me. I opened it and looked at the words my mother wrote on the first page: "Remember, son. You are never alone with Jesus at your side. It's his promise, not mine."

I pushed my head deeper into the pillow and let these words find room in my soul—that's the only way Jesus could be close to me.

CHAPTER 26

I woke up hungry and feeling refreshed in the morning. It's another day closer to going home. I answered the phone, thinking it might be Angela, but my Mother shouted, "Son, are you packed to come home?"

Peter, my youngest brother, shouted, "We are ready for you, George. Hurry up and get here."

I told her of Angela's great help, and "Yes, Mom, I am ready and getting a little excited."

"We are very excited on this end too, dear. All around us, the Christmas preparations are on people's minds. Everybody seems to be excited about George coming home."

"How cold is it, Mom? I don't know if I have enough warm clothes."

"Don't worry, George, your sister hung your warm stuff in your room."

"Mom, do I have to share my room with Peter?"

"No, he has his own on the third floor. He took over the whole attic and seems to love the privacy. No one wants to climb way up there to check on him. Here, Peter wants to talk with you."

"But, George, the door is open to you all the time. Come up, and we will have a few. I got a fridge full of it."

"You even got a fridge up there?"

"And lots of goods to eat too," he said.

I was imagining his smile and could not help but join. "OK, Peter, I'll see you soon."

"I can hardly wait. Bye for now, George."

Hanging up the phone, I wondered what Angela bought for Peter. *Well it is all wrapped up, nothing can be done about it now.*

I noticed my landlord Hans passing my window. I waved for him to come in. I opened the door for him. "Don't leave your shoes at the door. Come in, Hans. I just wanted to tell you of my trip, going home for two weeks."

"Great," he said.

"Is there anything I need to do in here before I leave?"

"Not really, George. I just checked outside under your window. The drains are open in case we have a heavy rainstorm or even more snow. You know, we had a hard storm last night. Lots and lots of rain."

"I must have slept right through it. Sit down, Hans, I will make some coffee, if you like."

"No, I just brewed some. I'll get you one."

In a flash, he returned with a bun and a mug of coffee.

"Great aroma," I said, holding a big mug over my nose. "What is the brand?"

"It's Jacob's Own. It's the only one to drink. You should take a pound or two home for your mom," he suggested.

We both made ourselves comfortable on the dining room table.

"How is life, Hans?"

"You know, George, I am really lucky with my tenants this year. You are a quiet bunch of students and leave no litter around. I am having it a little easier this year. Life is good, thank God. Regarding your going home, I should have your phone or address in the USA, just in case."

"Good idea. Angela suggested she should take my key, if you don't mind. You know her?"

"You mean that pretty blonde with those violet-blue eyes? What a charmer to have on your side. Keep her, man, she seems a down-to-earth, lovely person."

"Thanks, Hans, she is nice to be with."

Getting up, he mentioned doing some decorating outside.

"Let me help you, Hans. Let's get it done before another shower comes down."

"OK, I appreciate it George."

So we worked until noon, and just as we were taking the step-ladder to the shed, it started to rain.

We shook hands and wished each other happy tidings. Sitting in my favourite red chair, feeling good about myself being useful, I remembered that these are the same emotional responses I have when I do for the men arriving at the center—giving of my time, making somebody comfortable.

George, you have chosen the right occupation, and with that thought, I fell asleep and forgot to visit the center. I woke up at 3:00 p.m., hungry for a hamburger at Jess's place.

"That is a rare sight, you sitting and reading the news. What happened to your business, Jess?"

"Don't you worry about my business. There will be plenty of it tonight. Hi, George, come sit down here. It's good to see you."

"Tell me, what is special about tonight, Jess?"

"Town will be filled with people. There is a big sale going on, and folks end up here for a hamburger. It only happens the week before Christmas, and lots of people wait for this sale. It's like a street fair. Choppers, George, lots of folks come out, also school is out, and visitors. I am getting to be known as the best hamburger place in town. That is why I am working twelve-hour shifts."

"Good for you."

"Let's eat. Where have you been, George?"

"I have been busy since school ended. My brother sent a ticket for me to come home for Christmas, and I have been buying gifts for everybody."

"Heck, that sounds fantastic. When are you leaving?"

"I am flying Saturday morning, arriving home in the evening, and returning on New Year's on Monday."

"How great can that be? I tell you, some folks have all the luck smiling on them," Jess said, coming around the kitchen counter. Embracing me, he said, "Merry Christmas, George. I will miss you. I imagine you to have great fun being home with family." He went back behind the bar, and I sat at the bar watching him working his tools, turning our burgers.

"What about you, Jess? What will you do this season?"

"I work, making lots of money to be able to buy gifts and maybe spoil my girl Erna a little."

"Sounds good."

"The town looks so festive, you can't help getting into the mood," I said.

"Have you noticed that during this season, people behave differently, there is not a stranger around? There's so much love and hope floating everywhere you go. People from all over the world are here visiting families."

"I noticed that too, Jess. Why oh why, does it have to fade after the tree comes down?"

"It's amazing, George, every joint is packed. You don't know if you are drinking with a lawyer, doctor, a CEO from some big company, or a bum—everybody is your brother and sister. No end of hearing music of the season. It's big business, George. It's a different story with the older generations, the folks that were born here like Emma's folks. Mostly Catholic traditionally fill the church and eat at home with families. Like in Emma's house. They eat, drink, and tell stale stories."

"I sort of like it. It's just like home, Jess, but our village is quiet. The visitors we have are usually family from neighboring villages."

While we were enjoying our food, I wondered how I fit in at home. Bumping his elbow into my sides, Jess reminded me that brooding is unhealthy.

I noticed the two men walking by. "There, look, Jess, those tall guys. You see them? They were having lunch at the cafeteria yesterday, sitting at my table. Look at them now in uniform. I can't believe what I see."

"Recruiters, George, that's what they are—in need for cannon fodder."

"You're kidding me, Jess. I ate with them and listened to them talk about returning to the field. One of them has three kids at home and was going the third time serving his country, he said. I had a bad night because of it. I felt guilty being safe here."

"You are valuable, George, and these guys are looking for men like you. If they would have asked you yesterday to sign up, you probably would have signed your John Henry."

"No, I would not, but I am amazed that they knew my name and asked me if I was ready to return into action. The nerve of them coming into an area where men are not done recuperating from the first bout of fighting."

"I bet you these guys probably never seen action," Jess said.

Getting up he said, "How about a piece of apple pie with melted cheese or ice cream to celebrate Christmas?"

"Ice cream sounds good. Thanks, Jess. Hey, can I help you in the kitchen tonight?"

Looking at me, he said, "You crazy bugger. Sure, it would be great. But wait a minute, you are not insured with the company."

"What could happen doing the dishes, Jess? Let me, I'd be happy to do something."

"It would make me happy too, George, but first—desert."

Looking down at my pants, I said, "I hope I don't get these dirty. They're the one pair I have to wear home."

Throwing an apron my way, Jess said, "Good luck, and give it thirty minutes. It will start to get busy." Walking with him through the kitchens, he said, "George, remember, don't wait 'til your legs start to hurt sit down any time, you hear?"

"Yes, sir." I saluted.

Well, it became lively. It was 10:30 p.m. when the dishes finally stopped coming, and the three of us sat down for a beer. Emma had come to take Jess home and joined us for a beer. Smiling at me, saying, "You are the George that wants to stay in our fair town. What is it that draws you?"

"Actually, Emma, there are a few personal ones, but opportunity, the friendliness, being able to help my buddies are other attractions. I just feel like I am home."

"I am glad you feel that way, George. I was born here. I don't know if I had the courage to make such a transition. I hope Jess will stay here. He has a good chance working here, making a living for us." She turned around, shooting, "Isn't that right, honey?"

"Don't disturb me. I am counting money, honey."

All three of us chuckled.

We walked outside together. I noticed Emma holding on to Jess, looking up at him lovingly. *Nice couple*, I thought, *will someone ever want to hold on to me like this?*

I did not hear from Angela, assuming she was probably busy at home. Just before going to bed, she called, telling me she had worked at the center; some new wounded had arrived.

"Can I come with you tomorrow? Maybe I can help."

"I will ask and phone you, OK? Are you excited, George? Just two more days, and you are on Lufthansa."

"Angela, it appears that you are more excited than I am," I said.

I heard her laugh. "Could be," she shouted and hung up.

What a girl, I thought.

I watched some TV, and the newsmen were harping about what the Americans should do next in Iraq. But the Republicans, as usual, were against everything the Democrats proposed. Nothing else was on, so I looked at a magazine that I had pilfered from the center. The article "Moral Wounds" interested me.

Too many pages, I thought, *to start tonight.* It was written by army personnel with pictures of the writers in combat suits. *Courageous*, I thought.

I was reading something short and light when Angela called to tell me that Vivian wants to see me before I leave. She will find something for me to do.

"Want me to pick you up, George?"

"Thanks, I'll walk. Meet you at the cafeteria in the morning."

I washed the dishes I left in the sink from the morning and went to bed.

The wind felt strong and cool next morning, as I walked to open arms of Vivian shouting, hello, hello, my hero. What a pleasure to see you again. Don't ever go too far, George. I love you," Vivian said.

"I wonder why I gave you so much trouble when I first came hugging you."

"Oh, but look at you now, our success story. I hear you want to help. OK, come with me."

Turning to Angela, I said, "Where will you be, dear?"

"I go to the reception desk. Vivian walked with me to ER, and they will tell you what to do, George. I am tired and ready for bed."

While I was dressing into sterile gowns and covering my shoes, Vivian explained the patient's peril. "This young lad came last night. We don't know what kind of bacteria he brought. That is why you dress and you are not allowed to go into the other units. He is very confused and needs to be observed around the clock, George. If you want to give us a couple of hours' help to keep him safe, that would be good."

"What do I do?"

"Watch him. He's been constantly moving. Just watch he does not hurt himself. Maybe you talk to him quietly or touch him. It helped you a lot when you were like that. If you need something, push this button."

I listened to the mumbling as I approached the bed. "You look so pale, buddy." I inspected his childlike appearance. "I don't know your name. Anyway, mine is George." I looked around for a nametag. "Here it is. I read, 'Ben Wallace.' I like that name, Ben."

I stroked his arm gently up and down, while thinking of what I could tell him that would calm him. It was not easy to keep the covers on him. I noticed dressings all around his middle. "Maybe the covers are hurting you. I wish you could tell me."

I noticed an IV side on the side of his neck. "*Watch it carefully so he does not pull on it. Otherwise, he will bleed a lot,*" I remembered Vivian warning me. The bottle of fluid was right over my head.

"Oops. Good thing I saw that." I folded the covers at the end of the bed. "What else can I do for you, Ben, my buddy? I am sorry for what happened to you." I stroked his arm some more. I pushed some hair strands from his forehead and noticed the dirt and sand in his hair. My eyes filled up with water; I cursed and cursed those two deadbeat soldiers I saw yesterday.

I felt anger and hate taking its place, trying to possess all of me. Trying to control my emotion, I didn't know I was talking to myself, walking back and forth to the sink for clean wipes, taking out the sand from his hair.

Maybe it was the talking that calmed Ben down. I sat with him, put my head on the railing, and tried to calm the raging volcano in my soul. After a while, I looked and noticed that my patient was holding on to one of my hands. I folded a towel with my free hand on the rail and another one for my head so that I was not too uncomfortable as I sat there, squeezing his hand tied in mine.

You heard me, Ben. I am very happy. Ben, I want to tell you, you arrived in heaven on earth, and you will get well. Just believe, Ben. In a few days, it's Christmas. Celebrate, buddy, you are on safe ground.

RN Trudy came to take Ben's vital signs.

"Does Ben have family?" I asked.

"We don't know yet. He just arrived last night."

"Whom were you talking with so angrily?"

Not answering, Trudy said, "Well, it made Ben sleep. We cannot medicate him until we know what all is wrong. He is next on the list for surgery. Someone will come to take you to see Angela if you like. Vivian told me about you going home for Christmas. I am Trudy, by the way. I have to get this young man ready for surgery now. You have fun with your family and send us pictures. Merry Christmas, George."

"You have a good season too, Trudy. By the way, I can come back tomorrow or even this afternoon if you need me"

"Thanks." She waved.

I left my gown on the chair and walked the long hall toward the door. The sun shone through the large wall of windows, and the tall evergreens danced to the music of the wind. *It's nice here, feeling emotional, thinking—yes, I want to work here, relieving as much misery as I can.*

For the first time, I noticed pictures on the walls. *How could I have not seen them before?* Walking toward them, I realized how wide these halls were. I spent a few minutes wondering who these folks were who either donated or bought these paintings.

None looked commercial; there were some oils of animals and some in acrolith of nature scenes. I turned to a familiar voice and watched Dr. Kopp walking and talking with someone close by me. I gave a small cough, hoping he would turn.

"Son," he shouted, "what are you doing here?" He introduced me to Dr. Friedrich, not waiting for my answer. "A success story right here," he said to his colleague enthusiastically as usual. He invited me to watch a hip replacement from the balcony. "There will be other students of mine watching," he said.

I was astounded.

"Go get changed and get up there," he said, pointing to a balcony.

"Thank you," I said. As I walked toward a double door, I sort of ran toward a nurse, hoping she could tell me what I must do and where I needed to go. "I was invited."

"You lucky devil. Come with me."

We walked through the same door as Dr. Kopp did.

"Gentlemen, please help this person."

Some guys turned around and greeted me, others kept on talking. I felt uneasy, not knowing what to take from the shelves und stood undecided until one man paid attention to me.

"I am Dr. Henry," he said,

"And I am George."

"You are here on the invitation of?"

"Dr. Kopp," I said.

"Come with me then. Did you eat as yet?" Dr. Henry asked. "These surgeries can take hours, and you need to have a strong stomach for these bloody scenes. First time?"

"Yes," I said, having lost all eagerness for this drama.

"Tell you what," he said, "surgery is in one hour. We are being informed of the procedures. There will be a question-and-answer time for us. You have lunch during that time, just come back here, get dressed, and I'll pick you up. I know how it is. I puked all over myself the first time I watched this kind of surgery."

Feeling like a little boy on the first school day, I did what I was told and walked to the cafeteria.

My legs felt wobbly, and I hoped that I would not make a scene on the balcony with the other men, probably all of them being interns or doctors. I forgot about Angela, hoping she would not mind not meeting with her.

I was placed on the last bench. I had a good view, watching all sorts of people move around that large room. The walls were full of machinery, and tables were covered with green and white packages. Lights hung from the ceiling. I noticed one person going in and out, and they brought more packages. The other people were talking.

Finally, the patient on a Journey accompanied by the anestithiologist came into the room. The patient was on the respirator and placed in position the surgical table I noticed all kinds of tubes hanging around his body. Some packages were opened as the surgeons came in. I did not recognize Dr. Kopp for a while.

The man beside me pointed out what was going on before the actual surgery began. I heard Dr. Kopp's distinctive voice praying. I did not understand the words, but I saw folded hands. What I watched was very gruesome, and I had to close my eyes frequently and put my head on my knees. I heard orders given in anxious voices and then nothing.

I remembered each year we butchered a pig for the winter. We kids would watch how the butcher divided each hip from the body. This is almost the same, yet I knew under all those clothes was a person. I asked to be excused to catch some fresh air.

"Sure, just come back the same way. Are you OK?" Dr. Henry asked. "Or do you want me to come with you?"

"I'm all right, thanks." I stood against the wall to steady myself. My legs were cut off in the field, how did I come out of this so well without any problems? I did not want to go back to the balcony and told Dr. Henry.

"I don't blame you," he said.

Angela met me, bubbling about employment in ER starting January 15.

"Let's celebrate with ice cream. I'll pay."

Licking our spoons, she said, "How come you are so quiet?"

I mentioned where I had been. "Angela, I feel sick. I need to go home."

"OK, I'll take you."

I sat in my chair with closed eyes and was happy that Angela had nothing to say for a while. Later, I watched her look in the fridge to find something to eat.

"You like to eat tacos, George?"

"You know how to make tacos?" I asked.

"I make them all the time at home. I love to eat tacos."

"I don't know if we have all the stuff for it, Angela."

"We'll improvise," she said, and in no time, we sat at the table with a glass of milk and each had two tacos to eat.

"You want to look at your ticket to see when we have to drive to the airport and when you get to Oklahoma?" Angela said.

I took out the envelope my brother sent. "Good thing we did."

"Look here, we need to be there at least two hours before your flight. Will someone pick you up in Oklahoma?"

"I am sure, Angela. It will be great to see everybody, and yet I cannot explain the anxiety I feel."

"Are you afraid of flying, George?"

"Not really, but it's the meetings, greetings, and questions that I am anxious about, Angela."

"Remember, you have grown three years older, left as a teen and are now a grown man with a world of experience. You just might like being home so much that you don't want to come back here. They have nursing schools where you live too, you know."

I walked to the sink where she was washing the dishes. I turned her toward me and looked into her big, blue eyes.

"No, dear, I don't want to mess up again. Being here is a great opportunity. It is a beautiful area, and getting to know you and your family is God's gift, and I am grateful feeling part of the human society. Will you take my key and watch my apartment while I am gone?"

"Sure, I will," she said.

"By the way, I should empty the fridge tonight. Ms. Molly gave me so much stuff to eat."

"Don't worry, I will take home what might spoil, and the rest I will put in the freezer."

"Thank you. I don't know what I would do without you, Angela."

Suddenly, we were embraced and moving with the rhythm of the music on TV.

"I love you, George," she said.

Slowly, I pushed her from me, holding her at arm's length. I said, "Thank you, Angela. Remember, I am a cripple and poor."

"No, you are not, you are bruised, and bruises heal," she protested. "Stop that foolish talk now." She shook my shoulders as violently as she could.

"We will talk when I return."

Again, I said something I did not want to say. *What was there to talk about?* I wondered. *Am I getting into trouble here? Don't get too cozy, George.* Even so, it felt so wonderful. *Remember, George, you have nothing to offer to such a lovely woman.*

"Let's sit a little." I made myself comfortable, and Angela slipped right beside me.

"Move over," she said.

"There's not much room left."

"Let's watch the news a little," she said.

"I like German TV. There are no commercials between the programs, which is better to understand what is going on. Do you know who pays the bills, Angela?"

"Why, don't you have commercials after shows in the USA?"

"That's what I mean. We have so many, all through the news."

"You know, I never thought of who would pay for TV. I will know the answer when you come back," she said, smiling at me. Then she took my arm, folded it around her shoulders, and snuggled close to me.

We sat for a long time, quietly watching the day changing into evening. Suddenly, she sat straight up and said, "You need a bird-feeder out here for the winter."

"That is a nice idea. I will ask Hans if he can build one," I said. "What kind of birds do we have here in Germany?"

"We have the Eisvogel [kingfisher], Specht [woodpecker], Kuckuck [cuckoo], Kiebitz [northern lapwing], and Wachtel [quail] that I know of."

"Can you really tell them all apart, Angela?"

"I think so. Like the Eule [owl] goes 'u-hu.'"

"Oh, you mean owls?"

"And the Specht is very noisy when he pokes in the trees for food."

"And that is the woodpeckers."

"We have various kinds. Let me think."

I moved away from her.

"Kibitz and Wachtel have specific colors and peckers and are easy to differentiate from others. What kind of birds do you feed where you live, George?"

"I don't really know, just that I heard Mom talk about warblers, brown creepers, chickadees, and the blue jays."

"I remember in spring the swallows would make nests over the barn doors, and the Wanderdrossel [American robin] returning from I don't know where singing its heart out. Come to think about it, these two birds marked the arrival of the spring season. What did you like most about living on the farm, George?"

"My horse Ella. She always ran to the fence when I came home from school. Usually, I sat on the fence pole and talked for a few minutes. Her head would nod up and down at times. She would give one of her favourite sounds when Mom called to remind me to do my chores.

"I did not like hay time. The talk about weather and forecast never ended, and I hated the rush, bringing in the hay before showers surprised us. We rented a big machine, and neighbors would split the use of it. It seemed all I heard was, 'We need to do this or that.' Actually, that went on all summer through to the end of fall. Of course, I had to help, and I did not like it.

"How about you, Angela, what do you like about farming?"

"I like everything about living on the farm. I don't have to do heavy work like you did, but I keep the garden planted and weeded and bring some veggies in for dinner. I am not really assigned anything specific to do.

"In the fall, I empty the compost and help Grandma dig it in the garden. It's usually after a rain, and I liked digging the earth and smell it. I started it when I was a little girl. I just loved to be with my Grandma. Best of all, I like cherry-picking time. My big brother lifted me to the first big branch.

"From there, I climbed and ate cherries and sang my heart out. I still do. It's fun, George. That old tree brings the biggest and sweetest Bing cherries every year. You will see, George. I am very lucky living on the farm and having the city so close. To me, it's great, I would not have it any other way."

She moved her body deeper into the chair, and so the minutes turned into two hours at which point, Angela jumped up and said she had to go home.

"I am working the morning shift. It's not really work, but I am being trained in ICU."

"Are you being paid for that? That is pretty neat, you know."

"Well, I got to wait for a few more months, but I hope I can pick up a side shop after I become better organized with my time. Your time will come, George. As Grandma always reminds us, we should live every day as if it be the last."

"That is hard to do, isn't it?" I remarked.

"For sure, George, but for her, it is the only way to live. I am off work at four thirty. Oh, Mom told me to come get you for dinner tomorrow. She wants to send you of with a full stomach, I guess."

"Thank you, I will come."

"OK, I will pick you up after work."

"Thank you, Angela. I might go to the center and say farewell to everybody."

Getting ready for bed, I thought of how easy it was talking with Angela, thinking about how we had the same background and parents who guided each of us with their faith and integrity. I also became aware of how receptive Angela was to my earlier tenderness toward her. *How great it would feel for me to just let go and love her if I would have not been marred by this war.*

175

The next day flew by. I wished Vivian, Dr. Phillips, and my trainers a Merry Christmas. I ask Vivian about Ben recovering in the intensive care unit.

"I hope he will be up and on the go when you return."

We sat at the dining room and chatted. I was given phone numbers in case I needed them.

I walked to see Jess at McDonalds. He had just started his shift. We embraced like brothers.

"I am looking forward seeing you again, George."

"Don't forget to greet Emma for me, Jess. I will be back when school starts."

He walked me to the elevator, hugged me again, and said, "So long, buddy." He showed me a thumbs-up and was gone.

Man, it was an emotional day today, and it has not ended as yet.

Angela was on time, and the family gathered in the kitchen and dining room.

Joe came out of his office with a beer in his hands. "Let's have one together, George."

Just as noisy as at home, I thought.

There was some talking, some shouting, and chairs moving. I liked that feeling of comfortable, homely commotion.

Grandma Molly stood in the kitchen door with her arms wide open. "There is my boy."

I walked right into her arms as usual, thinking, *Tomorrow, I will walk into my mom's arms.*

The family was clapping and shouting, teasing, "Oma, you don't do that with us coming home."

"You all know I love you. Come, sit down. Barb cooked all morning."

"Oma, you sit at the head over there," David said.

"OK, and you sit there, Joe, next to George. I want to be surrounded by my grandchildren. Angela and her mother will serve us. What do you say, George?"

I had no words. I felt so many emotions. I vaguely listened to the conversation, thinking and hoping that Angela had chosen the right gifts. I must not forget to leave Angela's gift and January's rent money on the table in the morning.

We parted early. Ms. Molly asked if I had a warmer coat with which to travel.

"I don't think so," Angela said.

In no time, I was holding a winter coat on my arm.

"You probably need it tomorrow when you land."

Barb took my face in her hands and reminded me to spend lots of time with Mother. "She has waited for tomorrow a long time, George."

I promised that I would.

All were standing on the porch, waving; I felt like a celebrity. Hans was standing outside, and I reiterated that Angela would have the key for the apartment and the day I was returning.

Angela walked in with me.

"Let's see, George, if you have everything ready. Oh, you locked your suitcase? So we just put this here in your overhead luggage."

"OK. What else?"

"Your papers and tickets, great."

Walking her to the door, she said, "I will be here at 5:30 a.m. Let's see. You will be home in Germany at about 3:30 p.m. How exciting can that be, George?" She kissed me and jumped into her car.

I stood for some time and listened to the chimes of the nearest church. The bright ornaments of Christmas sights along the street looked festive. I walked to my apartment with all kinds of emotions that I could not explain.

How am I going to face my family? Why should that even concern me? Why does it? Why did I let my brother have his way in the first place, on top of it, paying for the ticket? How can I prevent anybody from seeing me on my stumps?

Within my family, there was no real privacy. *I wish I had a beer or two. George, you have done it again. You create your own trouble. If you were strong enough, you would have told your brother that you did not want to come home at this time. If you would be honest with Angela that you don't like her watching over you like a mother hen, you would probably feel better about yourself right now.*

So what the hell is the matter with you, George?

I turned on the TV and watched a program called *Best Mother of the Year Program.* It was a show of a family with eight children spending last year's Christmas in the alps. The youngest child was six and being helped by the mother. The rest of the children were placing things they wanted to take with them on the bed and fitting them into the one suitcase they were given. Watching this turmoil was hilariously funny.

The reporters asked the mother how she could keep so cool. She simply said, "How could worry help in this situation? Everything will fall into place." She said this with a smile and certainty.

Yes, I thought, *how all that worrying is helping you, George. Everything will fall into its place.*

I felt like lightning struck me. Suddenly, I was beginning to savor the moment of being ready to say hello to Mom and the rest of my family. My life is full proof of what this mother believed.

Everything will fall in place, just believe, George. Just believe.

With anticipation, I waited for Angela in the morning.

CHAPTER 27

I walked up and down the sidewalk to keep warm and happy for having the coat. I would have felt cold without it.

"There you are. Morning, George," Angela said, climbing out of her car. She gave me a quick hug, and she opened the trunk for the luggage. "Is that it, George? Let's go."

No one spoke for a while. Angela just peeked my way at times, smiling. When we saw the airport signs, "Frankfort Hahn," she said, "I need help now, George. Watch the signs with me. I don't want to make mistakes. It's getting busy already, and we are still thirty-five kilometers from were we need to park."

All went well. "This is big," I said.

"It's the third biggest airport in Germany and getting bigger. We have smaller ones, but Lufthansa does not fly there."

Standing in line, Angela turned to me, saying, "It is so exciting here. George, do you feel it too?"

"Yes." I smiled at her.

She grabbed my arm. "I wish I could fly with you."

"Morning, soldier, passport please. Going home?" the woman at the counter spoke to me. "Snowstorm in Oklahoma at the moment. One suitcase and one carry-on? Merry Christmas, sir."

I stood there befuddled. *Soldier—Oklahoma snow—all so fast. This woman has it all wrapped up in a minute, amazing.*

Angela tarring on my coat, said, "I cannot go any further with you, George. Security check's this way. Someone pointed to a large opening."

179

Still holding my ticket and passport in my hand, Angela said, "Don't lose anything. You will have to show that again, you know."

"OK, dear, thanks so much for getting up so early. Drive careful. Traffic will be heavy now. Say hello to the family for me."

"And you, George, you do the same. Enjoy the trip, and have fun with family and friends."

"Bye-bye. I'll call your mom's house when I get to my mom's."

Angela blew a kiss my way. Having my hands full, I just waved with my full left hand.

"This way to the USA, buddy," someone said.

The crowd became bigger and noisier, but a definite holiday spirit was in the air. The spirit affected me, and I began to feel confident about the trip home.

I was in line again.

"Open please."

Clumsily, I opened my overhead luggage. I was asked to take my shoes off. I did not know what to do. Everybody was taking shoes off, and I was slowing down traffic with my indecision. I informed the security officer that I have an artificial joint and prosthesis devise.

"Come around this way, sir," the officer said and led me around the checkpoint without having to take off my shoes. I closed my carry-on and walked to gateway G24.

A golf cart was driving beside me, and an elderly man said, "Buddy, do you want to walk it or hop in?"

I hopped in, and the driver smiled, saying, "Got to make life easy for a buddy, ain't that right? That is a long way."

"Thanks a lot." I looked at him, and I noticed an artificial hand on the steering wheel.

"Going home, buddy?"

"Yes, I am."

"The best place to be," he said, nodding his head. "Gateway G24," he shouted. "Merry Christmas to all." He turned to me, saluting.

I saluted him.

His large, brown eyes gave away a ton of history. He stretched out his right hand.

As I grabbed his hand, I held on for just seconds, conveying his spirit to me. Watching him driving through the crowd of people, I wondered what his soft eyes were trying to tell me.

I noticed the Starbucks Coffee sign. *These long lines for just a coffee?* I sat down, hoping that someone would serve me. I couldn't help think about the mother of ten children from the program last night. *For sure, she had the right attitude, but with ten children and everyone wants something different, wow—it must have still been a challenge.*

I had brought nothing to read, so I wandered through the magazine stands and looked at those beautiful models on magazines.

"Nice, eh?" Someone poked me in the side.

I moved quickly to another area, not wanting to be seen ogling.

"Why, George, it's all advertisement. Why don't you buy one to read in the plane?" the inner voice was telling me.

Five euros. Too much, I thought.

"Or is that a cop-out, not wanting to be seen with a woman's magazine?"

Well, maybe, I thought. *I am just shy when it comes to women and things.*

"First-class passengers boarding for flight 1798, Lufthansa to Oklahoma," the voice on the PA said.

Walking with other passengers to the counter, I noticed the same women who had checked me in, smiling at me, handing back my papers.

The stewardess pointed me to seat 12.

"First class?" I asked.

"Yes, sir."

"David, you are nuts. How will I be able to pay this back?" I muttered.

This elderly man at the window seat looked up with a friendly look, saying, "Good morning, young man." He pointed to the seat beside him.

After all the preliminaries explained, Lufthansa flight 1798 was airborne, and my seat partner opened his *New York Times*. Front page showed a picture of President Bush and Vice President Cheney calling for more troops to be sent to Iraq.

"Murderers," the man who sat beside me mumbled. He was busy reading the financials for a long time until his eyes sort of gave way, and part of the news fell to the floor.

I did not like that the front picture of the paper was staring at me, so I closed my eyes. *Yes*, I thought, *one could say "murderers."*

I was enjoying the service and food, but why do I always see a picture of my buddies in the ditch hollering or screaming or some covered-up woman with children running somewhere when I am comfortable? I have to get those thoughts out of my brain, but how?

I wandered through the plane to stretch my legs. I noticed two boys shooting at each other with toy guns, their mother dressed in a headdress watching them. I wanted to ask whom they were aiming at but was afraid they might say "Americans."

After I returned to my seat, the man next to me woke up and handed me the paper. "Here, son, I am done." He had difficulty climbing out of his seat and said, "Don't get old."

I read some of the political headlines and wondered why I had not picked up a newspaper from home that stewardesses offered as we boarded. Naturally, these headlines were all about Iraq reestablishing reasons for action, more troops on the ground.

"How do you like that sly smile of your president?" the old man who stood at my side inquired.

"I don't," I answered.

Sitting down with a huff, he said, "I cannot imagine how such a man could be voted for president. All those lies we were told, starting with his father. Hussein, yes, he was another Hitler and needed to be removed, but by their own people, not by us—the West," he said. "It is the greed of wanting the oil. Do you realize how many men we left to die in the sand and left the country in devastation?" he said.

I listened and wondered what would happen if he had been there.

"America, such a great country, but with so many blind people leading us."

I agreed with this person, but I did not feel like conversing.

After a while he said, "My boy, I need a little snooze." He asked the stewardess for a pillow and closed his eyes.

I was glad, not having to appear unfriendly. Realizing the great power of the president in playing with the lives of people and how devastating he has two more years to play in the White House, we will not have a friend left in the Middle East. As I read on, anybody disagreeing with him is faulted with something and was eliminated from his cabinet.

Do I discuss politics with my family? I don't remember ever hearing such talks before I left home. It will be interesting.

Looking at my watch, I was still a long way from home. I folded the paper and put it under the seat. Looking out of the window, there was nothing to see but white billowy clouds. I might as well relax, but my brain started to work and I felt old hostility creeping up.

"George, don't go there," Angela reminded me frequently to leave the past and look at the now.

Angela, you are right, I will be soon celebrating Christmas at home. I opened a magazine that pictured houses and tables decorated with their best—families dressed up, celebrating the season, the works.

I remembered all that preparing and decorating the month before. Mom knew in September which turkey she was going to cook, so she watched its food intake carefully. He was not to be chased by the dog. Christmas cookies filled tins; and the fruit cake, Mom's particular masterpiece, was placed in a special container. But I never liked the taste. "You don't have to eat it, George my boy," she would say.

My mom, I love you, Mom. There's a powerhouse, I thought.

Quietly, she took care of everything. We always had what we needed as kids, the house and the farm. She talked with neighbors when she needed equipment or another pair of hands in the busiest time during farmers' season. I remembered one night during a bitter, cold winter two cows giving birth to twins. *Four new calves at the same time,* I remembered.

Of course, everyone was excited about the good fortune. She carried one of the calves into the house and laid it in the bathtub. "Margaret, will you find some old clothes, and, George, you babysit with this little fellow."

As tired as she was, the porridge was served, and we got to school on time. When I think about her quiet, serene attitude as she worked each day given to her, I could only think, *Yes, my mother is a powerhouse.*

She did not have time to think of what the president or the world was doing. She took care of what happened on the day in her world. As we grew, we were given more chores to do, but it was always discussed at the dinner table. My mom would ask, "You think you can handle that?"

No one would dare to respond in a negative way. Probably, unknowing to us children, it might have been pure love and respect for Mom.

David would often help around the village like the villagers would help us. He would come home and tell Mom what he learned, and he talked like an adult while only being a fifteen-year-old kid. When Dad died of cancer, he stopped playing or fooling around with us and became a different person overnight.

I will see all of them soon, I thought. I felt a little fear and anxiety stirring in my soul. Arriving at dinnertime, I wondered who will be at the airport.

The elderly man beside me ordered a drink and invited me to join him.

A beer. A good idea. I thanked him.

He remarked on the good service in first class compared to what the folks got sitting behind us.

"You pay for it," I said and was thinking about David and his silliness of paying all that extra money. I would have been just as happy sitting somewhere behind. It will be some time before I can repay him.

As I lifted the glass to my host, I mentioned that I never drank a beer out of a glass. He smiled at me and sipped his martini. We sat quietly for a long while. Then while crossing his legs, he said, "I am glad to get home to my folks."

"Have you been gone for long?" I asked.

"Too long. Europe is so far ahead in the branches of medicine. It makes my head spin. I've been in it for many years and learned a fair share. It is refreshing and sometimes downright embarrassing to have young doctors teaching an old fox like me." After another sip, he went on to say, "My wife and family believe it is time to quit, but how can I close the door on all these men and women that are in need of treatment?"

Suddenly, I had an inkling that this man was someone who treated men like me.

Finally, his body turned toward me and said, "What about you, lad? Where did you leave your legs?" Our eyes met for some time. "Don't be surprised. Your shoes told me, son. I work at Oklahoma Clinic, therefore I am familiar with the tragedies of our men that come home injured."

I looked at my shoes and his too but could not see any difference.

The flight captain mentioned that we had crossed the Atlantic and will be arriving on time at Will Roger, Oklahoma, at 3:30 p.m. We exchanged another long look and smiled at one another.

"Merry Christmas, son. I am Dr. Helm." He stretched out his hands to me.

"Merry Christmas. I am George Reynolds. It is great to meet you, Dr. Helm."

The dinner was served like in a fancy restaurant. As usual, pictures of buddies helping themselves to a cigarette rather than food dampened my appetite. I closed my eyes and pictured them all. I wished I was with them at this moment but here on peaceful grounds. *What a Christmas that would be.*

"I am sure your folks will be at the airport," Dr. Helm said.

"Yes, I am certain. We live in Apache on a farm."

"I know the village well," he said. "I have good Irish friends that live there. The name escapes me at the moment, but we get the best apples from the orchard. Those people know how to celebrate. Everybody seems to be family. We used to take the children for a ride to see the lights during Christmas. You will have a grand reunion. Will you stay at home?"

"No, matter of fact, I will go back to Landstuhl in January, I attend school there."

"What a coincidence, I just came from there. If that is where you were treated, you had the best of care, George."

"I know," I said, nodding my head. I noticed a lot of dedication floating around there in every corner of the building.

"If you have time, come and see me at the Oklahoma hospital. I'll show you around. We try doing the same as Landstuhl, American-style."

"I might just do that. I sort of have to play it by ear. My folks want to do so many things in the short time I am home."

"I understand that, my boy."

"Another hour," I said, getting more restless by the minute and wished that all the fuss to come was over with.

"We must be descending," I said, noticing that the ground was white.

White Christmas, I thought. I read, *"Will Roger, OKC." Won't be long, George, for us to be celebrating.*

After a few announcements, the lights turned on. With a great commotion of people getting up, reaching for their bags, shouting good wishes, Dr. Helm stood in front of me, taking both shoulders and welcomed me home with a voice full of emotion. He shouted, "Come see me," as we were walking out.

CHAPTER 28

The fresh, cold air felt good as I was walking into the receiving hall. Not ten feet away stood my mom, and right behind her were a bunch of screaming people, lifting her off the ground as she was shouting, "My hero is home!"

All I could say was, "Mom, I love you."

We were asked to make room for other people; tears mingled with kissing, hugging, and welcoming me and did not want to stop. Peter asked for my baggage tag.

"Peter, you have grown," I said, looking at him, and in the same moment our arms folded around one another.

"It's been a long time, brother," he whispered in my ear.

Slowly, we ended up in cars and a truck for the short ride home. "Highway 62 had a lot more potholes," I noticed.

"There is a lot more traffic on that road now," David said. He was driving, and I was sitting beside him. He patted my knee and said, "Welcome home, George. We missed you."

I put my left hand on top of his right hand and thanked him for making it possible.

"Where is Margaret?" I asked Mom who was sitting behind me.

"She stayed home cooking and watching the baby. Wait 'til you see her. She is the happiest and prettiest doll."

My sister Margaret is a good-looking chick herself, and she is married to Brad.

"Lots of changes," I said.

"Yes, George, lots of good changes. You will see, and I hope you approve of them all."

As we turned into King Street, the lights turned on, and the bells from three churches were chiming.

"For you, George. Father Sebastian wanted it that way."

"That is very kind of him. I suppose we better go to church on Sunday."

"That is right, son, we better."

The house was decorated, and Margaret was standing in the front door with little Jessica. *I hope we bought a gift for her*, I thought.

As I walked toward her, that little hand of Jessica threw me kisses, and her little legs were busy kicking Mom's belly. Margaret set her down thinking that she walked toward me, but it was Grandma she wanted.

"How did you manage such a beauty, Margaret?" I asked as we hugged.

"With the right man," she said smiling, hugging, and swaying me all at the same time. "Remember, you never liked Brad when he wanted to date me."

"Well, he must have learned a lot to be good enough for my one and only sister."

"You will like him. You'll see. Come in, George, welcome home."

Everybody behind seemed to say and shout the same until David came in.

"It's time for a drink and relax. Are you all right with that, George?"

"Sure, I've been sitting all day, but if I could wash up a bit first…"

"That would help, of course. Come with me. I'll show you around to your room."

"You practically built a new house, David."

"Just added on. The family is getting bigger, and no one wants to move out. And this is your room. You can unpack tomorrow," he said, slapping me on the back. "Come, let's sit together. It's been a long time. Let's celebrate your homecoming."

Mom was still holding the baby, looking very happy to have all her kids under her roof. She put the baby on the floor and walked out to help Margaret in the kitchen. Brad must have come home through the back door. I watched him kiss his wife, and he stood in the door, having his arms around her.

"Look at us, you sinner, George. Do I deserve her now?" he asked, walking toward the baby with wide-open arms and laughing eyes. He picked the baby up, kissed her, and said, "Is she not precious, George?"

"She sure is," I said. "I hope we become friends."

"You will. Jessica loves everybody. Just like her mom when she was a teen. I had to keep an eye on her. She was so popular. I remember you were in the way all the time," Brad said.

One hurdle overcome. I remember how I made up stories about my sister for him to become disinterested, I thought.

The Christmas tree took up half the living room. I stood in front for some time and remembered some of the ornaments I used to hang.

"That is a tree from the corner of the apple orchard, remember, George? We had some problems with a bug a year ago and lost two of them."

"It grew a lot taller," I remarked. I stood back a little, inhaling the freshness and marvelled at how beautiful and straight it grew.

My thoughts wandered to Iraq and my buddies. *What are they doing at this time? It's the middle of the night their time.*

"What are you drinking, George?" David called.

"I am having rye and Coke."

"Sounds good."

"Easy on the whisky. I am not used to drinking strong stuff."

Mother came to stand beside me, her hand swiping over my back. "How are you feeling, son? You have been on the go a lot."

"Thanks, Mom." Looking into her blues, I couldn't help myself. I bent to kiss her warm cheek.

I listened and watched everyone's actions and the baby going from person to person, being admired and loved by all. Mother suggested to open a few gifts before dinner but got voted down.

"Let's eat, Mom, we are hungry," all said unanimously.

Everybody got up, and I heard the chairs moving in that big kitchen like in the old times.

"You sit where you always sit, George." David pointed to the chair close to the kitchen. "But tonight, you won't have to help your sister. She has her own man to help her."

It was all too familiar, and yet I felt alone. *I am home*, I thought, *where is that feeling that I cried so many times about in the field?*

"Let's pray!" Mother opened her hands, and everybody followed, joining hands and heads lowered. As always, Mom opens with praising the Almighty and ending with the same. I was looking at my family, and then Mom's eyes met mine. Maybe she wrote the thoughts of my heart and started all over, mentioning the staff in Landstuhl and the men out in Iraq fighting for our safety. I tried not to show the swelling of my eyes as I whispered my own words.

Mom and Brad got up and helped serve the food.

Yes, I am home, and it's good to be here with my family.

I could not move my eyes from Jessica in her high chair, eating every morsel that was placed on her plate with her fingers, making it known when there was nothing on her plate with her feet against the back of her chair.

We toasted frequently with a tasty white wine, and after a while I felt a comfortable heaviness that I had not felt for a long time. As usual, nothing escapes David. He suggested we open gifts in the morning.

"But that would interfere with breakfast and church," Mother said.

So, everybody wandered into the living room again. I went to get the suitcase that Angela had prepared for me. "Good, Angela."

As I opened it, Mother came to stand by my side. "A special card for Mom and one for the family," I said.

David was amazed at the English Angela used.

"She is an amazing woman, David, and was so much help during George's worst times," Mom mentioned.

"And I probably would not be here if it was not for her help. So, Mom, will you do me the honor?"

"Sure, George. I'd love to."

I sat down, and Mom read little stories that Angela wrote about the decision for each present. Also, the first one was for Mom, but she opened it last. Angela knew what my mother liked, and I noticed how she enjoyed looking at the little boxes of various perfumes and soaps of which Angela and I stood in front at the Kaufhouse in Landstuhl. I remembered we had fun that morning.

"Well, let's open," I said.

I forgot most of what we bought, stuff that they liked. *I spent lots of money that morning*, I thought.

Jessica was happy playing with the wrapping paper and didn't notice Grandma Molly's sweater that she knitted with a little hat and gloves.

David popped up, toasting to Angela, and asked me to show a picture of her. I have no picture of Angela, but Mom came to the rescue as usual and produced one.

"No picture of your girlfriend?" he said.

"Wait a minute, she is not that kind of a girlfriend," I tried to explain.

"What kind of a girlfriend is she?" Peter asked.

Mother lifted her hand and told the story of how much help Angela was to me while I recuperated. Mom explained that Angela was learning to become a nurse.

"So, tell me more," Peter said. "Do you have a girlfriend, George? I mean, a real girlfriend?"

"No, Peter, I have no time for a girlfriend. I am going to school and spend the rest of my time studying. Sometimes I visit friends at the center. That's about all at this time. On Sundays, I go with Angela's family to church. Somehow, I feel obligated to do so. They are a good family, also farmers, and I feel home there."

"You should," Mother got into the conversation for which I was grateful.

I did not feel like answering Peter's curiosity about life in Germany. I felt spent, and for the first time, my legs hurt. I could not tell which part of my legs gave me trouble, but it felt like the prostheses weighted a ton. I looked at my watch and all the gifts having to be opened. I sat down and stretched my legs, telling myself, "I can do this. I am home."

"Yes, Angela dear, you did a great job," I whispered in silence. Peter's shirt was light blue with a navy-blue tie. I remembered she asked me about the colour of his eyes that morning.

"Great, that is my New Year's outfit."

The picture frame for Brad and Margaret were well received.

It was late. Mom asked if anybody needed to eat something before going to bed.

"No, Mom, but let's have a toast and maybe call Germany. Wish them a good Christmas. It is morning there," David said. "I think we might forget otherwise because we are having a big day ahead tomorrow."

"That's good. Thanks, David."

"You want to do FaceTime, George?"

"I don't know, David, their schedule is just as rushed as ours in the morning. Just a short thank-you for now will be greatly appreciated by them."

I heard Barb's voice calling Angela and Grandma Molly to the phone. In no time, shouts of Frohe Weinachten (Merry Christmas} and thank-yous flew through that wire. I looked through the window, and it was snowing heavily.

"Happy Christmas, darling Angela," I shouted just before the line went dead.

"What do you mean she is not your girlfriend?" Peter asked.

I had nothing to say but just enjoyed the moment. Folks picked up their gifts, and I helped David pick up wrapping paper from the floor. Margaret walked the baby toward me to say good night. I picked her up, and she put those little arms around my neck and kissed me and said, "Night-night."

It was electrifying, the power of a loving child, her little fingers stroking my cheek. Walking to my room, I felt my eyes swell, remembering my buddy Joe. He will never feel his baby's love and vice versa.

Sitting on the bed, I did not know if I was offending someone when I closed the door, but I did not want anyone to see my tears. Also, I was afraid that Peter might come in, wanting to investigate my legs, and I was not ready for any explanation.

David knocked on the door. "Anything I can help you with, George?"

"I think not, thanks."

He stood over me, and then he sat down beside me, sliding his hand across my back. I just could not hold the tears back and let them fall.

"Sorry, I was just thinking about my buddies and their families. I am having a hard time letting go of these memories. Sometimes I even feel guilty for being so lucky and need to go back there to be with them."

"Don't go that far, George. You would still be there if you had not been injured. You did your deed. We are grateful you are home, and I want you to feel the same."

"I am trying. Thanks for everything. It is good to be home."

He walked out and closed the door. I was alone and hoped to be relieved from any more good wishes, as wonderful as they felt. I walked over to a chair by the window and watched thick flakes of snow dancing through the air. It was a beautiful sight with the Christmas lights outside. "I am home. I am empty of responsibility."

I rolled up my pant legs, took off my prostheses, but kept my pants on. *Will Mom show up as she used to do?* Sure enough, it was late, and I was in a comfortable doze.

She sat on the bed, looking at me, when she said, "Finally, you are home, George. You don't know how I waited for this moment."

I don't know, but when Mom's eyes looked at me, I see a certain depth—strength mixed with love coming from the very depths of her heart. I had seen those eyes when I looked into them from the hospital bed. I could never explain it. Here it was again, that eye contact I held until she got up and gave me a glass of milk.

"It's good to have you home, son. Sleep tight."

I was alone, changed into my pajamas, and brushed my teeth. The sheets had the outdoor smell as I got into bed. I wondered, *Is this my old one?* It felt good being off my feet, turning to the window, watching the snow falling silently as I fell asleep. I woke in the morning after an uninterrupted sleep and with the same picture of snow still falling. Hearing all kinds of noise, I wondered from where it came.

Looking out the window, I realized that I was downstairs in the guestroom, not in my old room. I got into my prostheses, a new shirt, and pants and walked to the kitchen.

Margaret was busy preparing breakfast. "So early. Morning, George. Come, sit, have some coffee with me. We had so little time to talk last night. I kept on looking at you and couldn't figure out what had changed. It dawned on me that you were just a kid leaving home and returned a man, a very handsome man."

"Well, you look different as well—so mature, happy, and more beautiful than ever. I used to be jealous of every guy that just looked at you. You were my only sister, and I was not ready to give you away."

"I remember that, George, but I am very happy with Brad. He treats me well and is a good provider."

"I see that, sis, and what a princess you have."

"Thanks, but tell me about you. I know about school and all that. You look so sad all the time. I just could not imagine you fighting in a war."

"It all happened so fast, sis. With all the stuff going on here at home, I did not think a lot about you. And when I did, my thoughts were often envious ones. You were seeing the world and getting an education, and the rest of us were doing the same old, same old at home."

"Mom was quiet, more serious than ever during your time fighting in Iraq. We did not know why because we heard so little of you. Did she have a premonition of what was going to happen? We talked about you at meals and wondered where and what you might be doing. I tell you, there was not a prayer said without mentioning you and the soldiers living beside you. A dozen horses could not hold her when we got the notice you being in Germany."

"Margaret, it was a blessing when Mom came, not only for me but also for the nurses taking care of me. I must have been a very angry individual from what I heard. I remember, if I had a gun, I would have used it. Yes, Mom was a great help, not for me alone but for the soldiers in general. She was a mom. Later, when I was in the wheelchair, getting around, Mom smiled and talked with other recuperating guys too. She was a mom to many."

"Yes, that is our mom. George, I better get cracking in the kitchen."

"OK, I want to help. Tell me what to do."

"No, you just sit and watch."

"No way. You used to like telling me what to do, remember?"

"OK then, let's get going. We need cups, saucers, napkins, and some serving spoons."

Mom showed up, watching us from the door, dressed in her heavy old coat that she wore going to feed the animals in the morning. She was smiling from ear to ear, wishing us a Merry Christmas. We embraced for a long moment.

"You still wear that old coat. I remember you wearing it standing at the stove, making porridge for us, Mom."

"I don't do the feeding of animals anymore. David does all the work, but I still like to go and open the stalls and feel the warm animal air. It's different, George. David is done by the time I get there, and I don't rush. I just enjoy that certain rhythm of the cows chewing their hay, the noise of the chickens, and when Ella was there, she would greet me with a special turn of her head. It's a good life, George. Enjoy while you are with us, son.

"Margaret, do you need me, or can I get dressed for church?"

"I am done, Mom. George is here. I will retrain him if necessary," she said, giving me the biggest grin and a pat on the back. I noticed a big smile as Mother walked out the kitchen.

"You turned everything around in here." I hunted for the correct utensils Margaret wanted to use.

"Yes, that's how it goes, when the big fish leave," she said, laughing her infectious laugh, showing her perfect set of teeth, coming to me with open arms. "I am so happy you are home. George, I'll tell you a secret. I just could not picture you being a soldier in Iraq. Also, I never told this to anybody, but I believed I had lost a brother. Remember you could not even fight that kid—what's-his-name—

who wanted to take your bike? I am the happiest person this morning being with you."

We embraced for a long time and together walked to the window, watching the wind whip the snow around that fell overnight.

"I bet it is cold out there this morning. Is it not beautiful, George?"

"Very peaceful, sis."

"By the way, you look great in this outfit. Did Angela help you with this?"

"No, matter of fact, this is her Christmas gift for me. I unpacked this morning. I like it too. I must tell her that it fits without trying it first."

"George, I believe that girl is the woman for you. Mom thinks that too."

"I don't know. I feel comfortable with her, but I am not in love with her."

"Here is a tip from your experienced sister—enjoy being together when you have the time. I mean, she must really care for you. You realize that much, do you?"

"Yes and no. She is affectionate, and I don't know how to take that. I am always wondering, 'Is that her personality with everybody?' because if she was in love with me, she should not show it like that."

"How should she show it then?"

"Heck, I don't know," I said, shrugging my shoulders.

"You will find out," she said.

Without saying anything, Margaret switched the knives and forks from left to right and left the kitchen, saying, "I've got to look at my two. Breakfast in fifteen minutes, OK?"

I watched David coming in from plowing the snow. His cheeks were red, blowing into his hands.

"Tomorrow, we do it together, David," I said.

"I only have one machine. There is a lot of snow this morning. I wonder how many folks will stay at home because of it."

Silently, I was hoping that were the case, omitting the dread of visiting with people I probably did not remember.

"Breakfast is ready," Margaret called, walking into the kitchen with Jessica, Brad, and the rest of the family trailing in.

"Come, let's eat so that we will not make Mom cross at us. You know her issue with punctuality."

Bacon and eggs, the usual food, but it tasted so good to me this morning. *Must be because of the eggs and the bacon probably from a close-by farm.*

Mom sat quietly, and Peter was determined I ride in his blue truck. What could I say?

"Let's go, George. I want you to meet my girl. She is gorgeous."

I looked at him from the side, wondering if I was ever that young. He was handsome, and I could imagine the need of feeding his ego.

"Let's go," Peter said. "Don't forget your coat."

"How long have you been driving, Pete?"

"Since you left, I think."

I could see the icy roads. "What is your hurry, Pete? For heaven's sake, you want to kill us?" I asked as we slipped from one side to the other.

"No sand on the road. That is why traffic is slow."

As we were waiting for the other family members to arrive, I felt a tap on my back. "Is that you, George?"

I turned and looked at Amy, my school friend and neighbor for some time. Just minutes after, guys with whom I played hooky arrived, shaking hands and shouting, "Let's get together, George!" It was great to see all these folks with whom I had grown up.

Mom came to the rescue, took my hand, and pulled me away from the crowd. I don't know where or how long Father Tomas watched the excitement.

"Good to see you on safe ground, George. Welcome home," he said, shaking hands too formally for comfort.

The mass was long, and I wondered about communion. *I have killed*, was all I could think about.

Margaret asked me if I would hold the baby.

"Gladly," I said.

It was a good distraction for a difficult moment, sitting alone in the bench, feeling all eyes on me. *But these people did not know how brutal I had been in Iraq. Would God forgive those brutalities? I know, if I had not used them, I would have been killed. Is that an excuse, Lord?*

At that moment, I made it my priority to discuss this very special situation. I sat there in deep thought until all people were seated again. More greetings and wishes came after mass. Peter was nowhere to be found. Mom said he'll be home when he gets hungry and told me not to worry.

"I was to meet his girlfriend," I said.

"You will," Margaret said.

"Let's get home. I have work to do," said David. "If you are dressed warm enough, George, I'll drive you a little around the farm."

"Let's do that, David, and see all the new things I've heard about."

We let Mom out at the front door, and David and I drove around the farm.

"You cleared all that snow this morning, David?"

"Yes, I did."

We were passing a new barn with a red roof.

"That is our garage for our farm equipment. Remember when we had to ask neighbours to borrow their stuff, George? We bought one piece after another as we could afford it. I took Mom shopping with me each time. I enjoyed that a lot, and she did too. As a kid, I always promised Mom, someday, we would have all the equipment we needed. She would just smile at me."

"Man, you worked your butt off, David."

"You know, George. I love doing what I am doing. Truly, I am happy being outside and farming."

"When do you have time for a wife and some children, brother?"

"That is next, but good women are hard to find. Mom thought I should take a vacation to Germany and look around. Besides, she loved it there, and I've been thinking about it. I am trying to get Peter to take a more responsible part in this farm, but he shows little interest. He is thinking of joining the Marines. Mom will have a fit when she hears that, I know. It is still a secret between him and me.

"Margaret's husband is helping out a lot. I don't think I can ask him for more time here at home. Brad is a real fine person and a great family man. I don't have to ask him. He knows where and when he is needed. We work great together."

Walking around between all the machinery, I felt a deep respect and pride in my eldest brother and had to tell him so. "David, you held it all together here at home while I went to fight a war that should never have started."

Our eyes met for a long minute.

"You have no idea what is going on there—the propaganda, the lies, and deception. I was blinded, like so many of my buddies. Like me, I did not sign up for the army to fight. My motivation was to improve myself and be of use to the world. I remember I was called a sissy by the boys in grad school because I could not shoot a rabbit. I came home with many a nosebleed because one of my buddies were bullied. Helping him meant I received a bloody nose.

"Look at me now, David, I have become a killer in the worst way. I could not go to communion this morning because I shot I don't know how many civilians because I was afraid they would kill me first, if I were not fast enough. Fear, screaming, and running—no time to ask questions. We are destroying the country of Iraq and dehumanizing its people. In the meantime, we are maiming our men and women with drugs, and so many soldiers play with the thought of suicide.

"I am lucky, very lucky, to be here in one piece. So many guys I listened to while I was getting back on my feet telling horrid stories of high-ranked officers losing faith. So many soldiers take dope to go on in this daily mess."

David sat quietly and just listened.

Sitting by the opening of the garage door with the sun and the brilliance of the snow made this day perfect. We heard the church chimes playing "Let There Be Peace on Earth," telling us that it is noon.

"George, Mom will be looking for us soon. Let's go see what is happening around the house."

"You mind if I walk to the house, David?"

199

"Heck no, I will walk with you."

We passed some tree stumps, and I tried to remember what kind of trees they were.

"We used to toboggan over there."

"You are right, and here stood the Christmas tree. Don't worry, down under, we planted about thirty more. We have room for twenty more in the spring, George."

"By the way, David, I met a Dr. Helm on the way home. He came from a seminar at the center and lives in Oklahoma."

"Amazing you would meet him."

"Yes, he sat next to me. Anyway, he wants me to see him at his VA center."

"You think we could do that?"

"I would like to compare Germany's and our VA hospitals. He believes that Germany is far advanced with techniques and treatments."

"Should be interesting, George. Maybe a few days after New Year's, we will plan a day to meet with Dr. Helm."

We heard Peter's truck driving around the corners. He jumped out, hollering, "Well, if you guys are late for lunch, I have nothing to worry about."

"Where have you been all morning, Pete?" David asked.

"Just with my buddies. It's Christmas, you know, a day to celebrate. George, what do you think of the farm? Did our brother show you all the machinery we bought?"

"They must be great fun to drive, Pete, can you drive all this equipment?" I asked.

"Not yet, but soon."

David and I exchanged eye contact, understanding each other's thoughts.

Peter was not meant to work this farm, so how is David going to get away and go on a vacation? I wondered.

As Peter jumped back in the truck, we closed the garage doors and walked toward the house, preoccupied with our own thoughts. The aroma met us shortly before the door. A smiling Mother met us at the door.

"It's all ready for a hungry bunch," she said, patting our arms as we met.

I admired the beautiful table setting and asked if Margaret did that all herself.

"Well, you were nowhere to be found, George. But you know, I enjoy doing that, except it does not last long and no one seems to even notice except you."

"Margaret, the table really looks great, but you see, the food you cook takes priority over the setting and you hear daily how we love to eat what you cook, so please don't be too offended," David came to the rescue for all.

"I know, just kidding, David," she said.

So we ate, laughed, and cracked jokes.

It seemed that when I experienced any homely pleasure, I was reminded of someone less fortunate than I was, like the wheelchair in the doorway, greeting me in the hospital and telling me he was going home without arms and legs. I could not imagine what this family had to go through day in and out. I felt grateful for having met this soldier because it was his daughter who opened my eyes to my great fortune of having hands.

I can be useful with my hands, I thought, imagining that that man wished he could be holding, loving, his children, and helping his wife with daily chores. That was real hardship.

Even so, I got up early, but David was working when I got outside. I blamed it on having to strap on the prostheses. The lights were on, the door was open, and as I got closer, I could feel the warm air coming from inside.

"David, do you think the animals would respond to me the same as to you if I would come in before you?"

"I don't know, but if you want to try it, go ahead. Maybe I turn around once more in bed tomorrow."

"I got an idea." Peter popped up. "I am sure these dumb cows will turn if you put on Mom's coat," he said, laughing at his own joke.

I enjoyed working beside my brother and remembered how I hated when he told me to help in previous years. It was the stillness, the slow moving of the animals, as they moved toward the door into the cold. We cleaned the stalls together. Peter vanished into thin air. David took time to explain where he would grow the corn and weed and what fields needed to rest.

"You are so organized, David. Did you learn this from Dad or Mom?"

"I think I learned a little from both. When Dad died and Mom had to take over, she would never say what we were going to do. Mom would ask me, 'Son, what do you think of doing this or that?' as so I was Dad. Dad always knew what to do and how to say things in a firm but loving way."

"You know, David, I do not remember too much about him."

"Yes, you were a small kid when Dad died, but I remember he'd carry you on his shoulders and Pete in his arms coming in the house shouting for Mom to watch her children."

New Year's Eve came too quickly. Soon after dinner, Mother assembled everybody to go on Skype with Angela's family. Ms. Molly, Barbara, and the men seemed to be in high gear chatting, laughing, and celebrating the first hours of a new year. Angela especially seemed to be in a happy frame of mind.

"I can't wait for you to come home, George."

"It won't be to long from now," I said. "Hi, Joe, I want you to meet my big brother. He plays with the same machinery you do."

"Hi, David. Cleaning up time for these monsters over here."

"We do the same here, Joe. No rest for a farmer."

"You're right, but I wouldn't have it any other way."

Ms. Molly came into the picture, shouting, "How is my boy?"

My mother shouted back, "Thank you for taking such good care of my son, Ms. Molly. George speaks of you many times."

David whispered in my ear, "Man, is she a beauty."

"I've never seen her like this. I think she is tipsy," George said.

"Don't you wish to be with her now, George?"

"Not really, David. I am where I want to be—with my family. It's morning in Germany, and they are probably getting ready for some bacon and eggs, and we are waiting for the big number 12—midnight.

"It's amazing how our family is so very alike," I said. Both practice the same religion, both make a living of farming, and even both husbands died young and the moms had to take care of business and families. Yet we're living an ocean apart.

Mother added, "My son should be lucky enough to meet these nice folks."

"Yes, Mom, I am very lucky."

"All because of meeting Angela," she said.

"Incredible. A miracle."

After a while, Brad brought out more food and champagne. Neighbors had gone after spending some time wishing good tidings for the new year. Mom had gone to bed, and Peter was at a party. It had become quiet in the living room. Margaret's head was leaning against my shoulders.

"Are you ready for bed?" I asked her.

"No, I want to party, just the four us. Just think, George is leaving us in a few days." Her eye swelled with tears.

"Good God, here we go. My little sister is tipsy too, like Angela." I got up, took my sister by her hands, pulling her from her husband, and held her tight in my arms, rocking with her to the music and noise from the TV until the moment of countdown.

The rest jumped up, and all four counted down, "Nine, eight, seven, six, five, four, three, two, one, zero! Happy New Year!"

We were all on our feet enjoying the moment. Someone turned the TV off, and we ate more food and another bottle of the bubbles.

"On a more serious note, George. Do you want to go to school in Germany? I mean, if you are not in need of the center anymore, why are you there? I mean, we have all the schools you need, not very far from here."

After a pause, I tried to explain that it was the center that I liked because I felt close to the wounded who feel strange and confused during the first weeks.

"I believe I can make a small difference in their recuperation. David, you should come for a couple of weeks, be with me, and see what I mean. It is hard for me to explain what it is like waking up and looking into strange faces.

"I had Mom making all the difference in the world, but most of these men have no one. For weeks, I did not know where I was. I was very fortunate that Angela was assigned to me during her volunteer work. So, yes, being there, I can maybe help these guys. Well, David, you will understand when you come."

Margaret and Brad thought that to be a great idea, David taking some time off from the farm. "Now is a perfect time. Nothing Brad and I cannot do on the farm at this time of the year. Don't you agree, Brad?"

"You are absolutely right, dear."

"Don't come home without a wife," Margaret slipped in.

David broke off the stillness and reminded me that I wanted to see the VA center in Oklahoma.

"What do you want to go there for, George?" Margaret said. "It is not a nice place to see, I hear."

"So many complain of how these poor vets are treated. It takes a whole day to get there and back."

"Please, George, stay with us. The time with you has been so short," Margaret continued. "I think you should rethink going to school here at home, George?"

"As I mentioned, over there, I am close to soldiers being flown in and I can help nurses. I feel these buddies, like when another buddy got through the hardship, they will get through too. Nurses think I give them hope. I like being involved. About visiting Dr. Helm, maybe we could telephone him so I'll spend a few more days at home."

"Great, let's drink to that."

Mom appeared at the door. "What a noisy bunch of kids."

We all jumped up to wish her a happy new year with yet another toast.

"Those were good days, Margaret, but it is time to pack." I cushioned the jams, preserves, and boxes of homemade bakery in my suitcase. "What if I have to leave that all at customs, Margaret? You know that stuff is not allowed."

"You came with a suitcase full of stuff that was not allowed, remember? Don't worry, it will be all right."

"OK, if you say so."

David promised seriously to think of taking that vacation.

CHAPTER 29

New snow had fallen, and we all sat in the kitchen the morning I was to fly back to Germany, when Peter came running in the house, saying, "Sorry, George. I've been so busy, I spent so little time with you."

"It's OK, you are still my favorite little brother. I was young once too." I held him close, loving him, and he somewhat felt embarrassed.

With tears in his eyes, he said, "I love you too, George."

Everyone wanted to say farewell at the airport. Even little Jessica was going to see Uncle George away. The goodbyes were not as easy as the hellos.

As I turned one more time, I noticed tears in everyone's eyes. Walking through the gate, I was encouraged for a year of hope and success for my family. I felt most certain I was the receiver of the best wishes and gifts in the world. *I am blessed with a loving family.*

I did not feel so bad about sitting in first class this time. I understood that paying for it was not a hardship for David; rather, it was love for his brother. I thought of Mother, remembering her role during hard times in teaching us quietly, but each daily step she took and words she spoke were thoughts before they came out of her mouth. *Mom, you are my hero!*

As I made myself comfortable in my seat, I thought of David, the eldest of us. I believed him to be like Mother in many ways. *Yes, brother, I do pray that you will come to Germany during my second semester break and spend time resting and enjoying the company of my German family, and, brother, I will repay you for the wonderful reunion at home with my family.*

The flight was uneventful.

As promised, Angela was waving a flag, meeting me at the airport. Hans had lit a fire, and the apartment was inviting. I embraced Angela and thanked her for her help with the gifts and how everything was well received.

It felt good to be in my own place. We ate a sandwich and shared a bottle of beer. Angela noticed my fatigue and asked if I would like a pickup for church in the morning. I agreed to go to the later mass. With that, she bid me good night, and I was finally alone.

I collapsed into my red chair and reminisced about my homecoming for which I had so much fear. Again, thinking David being here with me for a few weeks will be great. I had warned him that I would have little time if he came while school was in session. In any case, there were lots to see here, and language was no problem.

I awoke feeling cold as the fire was out, and I got ready for bed. I noticed the message blinker on the phone. *Who would phone me?*

I fetched a pen and pad in case I needed to remember a number. The caller spoke with a soft voice, addressing me.

"George, you do not know me, but I know you well. Joe, my late husband, spoke of you in his letters as you being his best friend. I wondered how you were doing and recuperating from this terrible night. I live with my baby, little Joe, here in Kansas City. I was curious of what you might know of my husband? What you talked about during the last days of fighting together? I miss him terribly. Life would have been so good. Little Joe looks just like his dad.

"For a long time, I thought that you had lost your life with him. Another soldier living not too far from here with his family on relief reported that you were critically wounded and flown to Ramstein, Germany. I hope you have recuperated and maybe live at home with family. It would be nice to hear from you, Ann."

Speechless, I listened to the voice and remembered Joe mimicking her voice frequently with a smile at moments of rest in the trenches, telling how cute she was at only five feet tall but could be stubborn like an ox. I listened again to the whole message. *Do I want to meet you, Ann? Yes, I want not only to meet you, I want to love you and care for you.*

I felt an immediate affection for Ann so normal to me. I sat back in my chair enjoying these new emotions. I felt her warm body so close to mine, her arms around my neck, the sensation rippling all the way down my body like a pebble thrown into a pond. *That is love. I have found my love. I am in love with Ann.* I pictured Ann's nestling head against my shoulders and her whispering sweetly confirmed to me that she felt the same.

I jumped up, hoping that I had not cancelled out the information. I listened to the message once more and wrote her phone number on paper. It was 4:00 a.m. in the morning. My suitcase looked at me to be emptied, but I got ready for bed thinking how early I could call Ann. *I need to hear her voice again, but what am I to say to her? I cannot offer her anything. I am a man without legs.*

Looking at my stumps, desperation awoke inside of me. The night was short and my sleep restless, but I was ready for Angela when she came.

Nothing had changed in her household. As usual, I was received as part of the family. After the hugs and kisses from the ladies, I had to tell how I felt being home. Of course, there were many questions about the business of the farms, and Grandma Molly wanted to know if I was thinking of moving back home. I wondered why she would be so interested, but I did not pursue the answer.

They enjoyed the pictures we sent and just now could imagine how big the farm was. I shared with them that my brother might come this winter for a visit. "That is exciting, and Angela wanted to know his age and if he was married."

I told her about the conversation I had with my brother about his accomplishments while I was gone. I had mentioned he should look for a wife and have children. He agreed. That's when I suggested visiting Germany, that the women are very pretty.

"Is your brother as handsome as you, George?"

"He is much better looking, plus he does not have to take off prostheses before he goes to bed," I said.

I was in a hurry and I excused myself after lunch, but within minutes, Ms. Molly had prepared a lunch to take home. I did not give a reason for my leaving because I had no idea how to explain my strong feelings to call Ann. I was hoping for a reply from the message I left that morning. Angela was on nightshift and wanted to rest before she had to go to work. All worked out well.

"I'll drive you home, George, because I want Angela to go to sleep," Barbara said. I was pleased with that too. Angela would have probably stayed a while.

Finally, I was alone. It was 9:30 p.m. in Kansas. *What the heck am I going to say?* I was nervous dialing that long number and tried it three times before I got it right.

"Ann speaking," I heard her say.

"Ann, this is George—Joe's friend."

I heard nothing for what seemed a long time. Then she said, "George, I have to put little Joe down. Just a minute."

After another long wait, I heard what sounded like snivelling and asked if she was OK, and she said, "I am so happy you called, George, and hope you can tell me more about my Joe. I know he was a buddy of yours. Toni, who broke up the argument between you and Joe about who should go on patrol that night, apparently, he broke up the argument and suggested that both of you go."

"Toni… hell yes he did. He was sort of the daddy to us because he was older or appeared to be. My goodness, that is great that he is home."

"But, George, he is thinking of returning to be with his buddies. Of course, his wife is totally against this. It would be the third time for him—such dedication, just imagining it. I miss my Joe so very much. Although I am grateful I have the baby, he is truly a delight, but still.

"The in-laws, Joe's mom and dad, tell often that this little man is just like his father. It helps when they come and tell me that. They are both good to me, a comfort. I am doing OK, in general. How are you, George? Are you going back to fight?"

"No, Ann, I lost both legs below the knees. No, I am not going to fight anymore. But I do think about my buddies that are over there and in danger every minute of the day and night. I understand why Toni wants to be with his boys, as he called us. Believe me, Ann. He was a great help when courage was shortcoming. He got us going, dead tired or not. All of us gave what we could and fought together. But then they are his family. It must be a very difficult decision for him to make."

"George, I do not know. Are you in a wheelchair?"

"I am walking with prostheses and have no problems, but every night I am reminded of this crazy war with going to bed without my legs." I noticed the long pause on the other side, wondering what Ann might be thinking.

I was relieved when she asked, "Are you still at the recuperation center?"

"No, Ann. I have my own apartment, and I'm going to school here in Germany to become a nurse. I want to be close to the wounded buddies that are flown in from the field to be treated."

"That must be hard, or do you know the German language?"

"The town speaks English, Ann. This is a town that is built by Americans. It is an interesting story. I will explain it to you sometime, but I need to get ready for the first day of school after the holidays. I will call again, if you like."

"Oh, please do so, George."

"I will, Ann, soon."

"OK, good night, George."

"Bye for now. Blessings to you and little Joe."

I hoped that I did not make a mistake by being so short. I had the need to be alone with the thought of Toni returning to this unnecessary bloodshed. He was always such a levelheaded guy; the group would always listen to him when he spoke. I liked him, and so did my buddies. He would be welcomed in the army for sure, but would he return to the same group?

Toni, stay home, I thought. *I should have gotten his phone number. So what? I still could not help him. I understood his sentiments about helping his boys, as he called us. I had these same strong feelings frequently, lately being saved and having no problems walking. I probably could find something to do over there behind the action, considering that I had no problem with walking and otherwise a fairly healthy individual. I am very grateful I can walk again, but to go back, no way would I do that.*

On the flight home, I had read an article about a mother having lost her only son and, in her pain and anger, she wrote an article accusing the president of being a murderer and telling nothing but imaginary stories of how we could lose our freedom in the USA due to the weapons that were stored and could be used by Saddam Hussein.

She explained that the war machine was a cruel business and human bodies such as her son's and many other young fathers and sons were being used to enrich the already-wealthy individuals. This grieving mother thought that there should be provision in the registration paper for the young men or women not wanting to serve in active duty. A safe statement of objection should be written in the application without being penalized for being immoral or unethical.

But as I understand it, it is illegal for refusing to fight, even in an unjust war, whatever. Belief of the individual is not honored. Frankly, at this point, I do not feel any disloyalty to the country, but I do experience emotional empathy for my buddies and actually see them tired and weary in front of my eyes.

I wondered what Toni would say about this woman's thoughts and beliefs. He was always ready to boost our morale with words of encouragement.

I ended up in my chair with a beer. The news of Toni wanting to return to Iraq gave me no peace. He was on leave, knowing that his family were safe at home and thinking about the men fighting.

What a guy. I wish I could talk with him, get to know him in his private life. But that was not feasible. I need to think about school that started tomorrow. I have no idea how to prepare. No books or assignments as yet. Funny, Angela did not discuss anything about school with me. I need to find my own way. This is complicated without Angela, for sure.

Again, I realized how much help that woman was in my life. She did so much for me without me recognizing any of it. *George, you have got to do something about that, but first I had to find some sleep. The morning would be here soon.*

As I was removing my prostheses, I thought of Ann and what might go through her head at this moment, *Me being a man without legs and walking on these damn prostheses? Well, George, you will find out in time.*

CHAPTER 30

I walked to school the next morning. I noticed big tables outside and lots of men and women gathering around. I went to a table with a sign saying, "Second Semester," and found my name with a card telling me where to go for my books and schedule.

Easy enough, I thought.

I went for my books first, which became very heavy while walking to my classes.

An elderly man stood in the door of my German language class. "Morning, soldier," he said, "finding everything?"

"Yes," I said, "I am George Reynolds. Are you the German teacher?"

"I am, son. I am Pete Peterson. We will get along fine and don't you worry." He gave me a pat on the arm and walked past me.

I sat on the first bench I could find, and the aroma of fried food made me feel hungry but I needed to rest first. Thinking about the books that I had to carry each day without meeting Angela worried me a little. *It will be different this semester.*

I felt lost and lonely; even so, there were many people walking all around me. The first couple of days at boot camp came to mind. I felt the same emotions. I sat trying hard to think of the positive difference now, but nothing came to my mind. I seemed to have lost my appetite.

Just watching people passing by, I saw Angela coming around the corner, shouting, "I thought you might be getting hungry by now, George."

"What a heavenly surprise you are. How did you know I was here?" I ran toward her, hugging her, squishing the hamburger and the drinks. "I am so happy to see you, dear."

"Well, with that welcome, I feel on top of the world myself. Here, take these burgers and sit. I have to get some paper towels to dry myself a little."

As usual, nothing is a big deal for Angela, and in no time, we sat and enjoyed the food and I the company of my dearest friend.

"It was kind of quiet at work and I don't feel tired, so I thought about you. Wondered how you were making out on your first day of school," she said.

"Let me see, here are my classes and the names of the teachers and schedules." I showed her.

"Do you know any of them?" she asked.

I gave her the paper, and Angela scrutinized the schedule.

After a while, she said, "You know, George, you will find that this semester is very different. There will be a lot of introductions to medicine and going to different areas of the hospital, making beds, and watching procedures like how to turn a patient, functions of beds, and all the instrument hanging behind the bed."

I was puzzled and said, "I would think that this stuff would come later."

"Yes," she said, "but in the third semester, we had a patient, and you have to know all the nitty-gritty stuff before that. Anyway, that is what we did in my second term. We did a lot of walking, I remember, through units like medical and postoperative units. We had to dress in sterile gowns to walk into an operating room and sterilizing area. You know, there are lots to know in that room."

I was amazed. "These people that work in the sterile areas have to know all the instruments that doctors use for specific procedures. Then these sometimes little tools are being folded and marked for the many different kinds of surgery. The runner in the operating room has to be quick to fetch the specific tool that the surgeon shouts out."

After sitting for a while, poking me in my sides, she said, "If you are done here, I can drop you off at your place. I am getting ready for my nightly sleep."

Watching her, I asked if she had problems going to sleep during the day.

"You know, I was warned about that," she said. "But it makes no difference. I fall asleep as soon I get to bed."

Walking toward her car, she told me that she gets very sleepy around 4:00 a.m. "I really want to go to sleep then. But that is usually the beginning of the busy time for nurses. Patients waking up and in need to be turned or medicated or vital signs are taken and reports are written. Some nurses wash their patients. Some doctors come in early for their visits, and we give reports to them. I like that part because I can tell them myself what happened with my patient and usually have a question or two for the doctor."

"Thanks for lunch and taking me home, Angela. I really appreciate today. I did not have a good night and feeling not all together."

"How come?" she asked.

"The night was too short, for one thing, and I was thinking about Toni wanting to go back to Iraq."

"Who is Toni?" she continued asking.

Whoops, I thought, *I wonder if I should tell Angela about Ann's phone call last night.*

I told her, "Toni is a guy that was wounded just before he finished his four years of duty. He came home on leave and wants to go back to that hellhole. What bothers me, Angela, is that he is leaving four children."

"Wow, that would be a hard decision to make. What about his wife? Does she not have anything to say about this?" Angela said.

"Apparently not, Toni believes that he needs to be with his men. You know, Angela, I know what he feels. I feel the same way sometimes, wanting to be with my buddies, knowing what they are going through."

Looking at me, she said, "Really, George? You are still playing with that idea of going back?"

"I did not say that I was going back, dear, but I am thinking about the guys all the time."

"I hope that will fade in time, George, and I believe it will when you actually work with the wounded. You're going to have lots of other things that will occupy you this semester. Have a good week at school, and don't be afraid to call if you need me."

"Thanks, dear," I said, getting out of the car, waving.

I was relieved that Angela did not come in. I needed to be alone and look at my books, getting my mind into action about school. As I checked the classes, I realized that I had to take all these books each day. Even though I lived close to school, it will be challenging, especially during winter. *I have to be very careful not to fall*, I thought.

The afternoon sun shone warm through the window, and I felt content in my apartment. *It will be nice when David comes.* After watching some TV, I promptly feel asleep and woke up late again. As I was getting ready for bed, I thought of what Ann would have to say watching me getting out of these prostheses.

Well, George, you are really jumping. We spoke the first time on the phone, and you are already going to bed with her. Ann lives in the USA, and I am penniless and live here in Germany. Why was that voice on my mind so often? I realized that I could not even look into the bathroom mirror without my prostheses.

Either I put my legs on again, or I will shave in the morning. This limitation, you have to live with all your life, George, nothing would change that. A marked man, that is what I am, even the German teacher called me soldier. How the heck did he know?

I wondered what he was thinking of these crazy Americans fighting this war. Somehow, we never discussed the war at Angela's house. Yet the whole town was built to help recover the wounded, looking at this town being built on the backs of human suffering. The airport and the hospital were built to get the wounded out of danger without having to transfer them to other hospitals in Germany. But as the century-old story goes, greed wants more greed.

Big factories for building war equipment are constantly producing bigger and better equipment to be sold and bought by countries. They need to be in constant use to kill people and damage the earth. There are many writings, stating, if the West would not have invaded the East and started the war, we would not have to go through this entire trauma

I guess the people living here had to agree with making this little, quiet town a human rescue station. The best surgeons and doctors from anywhere in the world come here and work. Many stay to live here, enjoying this culture and nature. The building boom is flourishing—the airport so handy for travelers and the shops for the wealthy and not so wealthy that come from all over the world to visit family members who where injured.

It is being said that the best surgeons are employed here to recuperate these men and women. Maybe that is the reason for nobody talking about the outrageous devastation of cities in this whole region of Afghanistan and Iraq. *For what else, but the oilfields?*

We know it was not for the safety of our country. Unless one has seen the killings of women and children and the maiming of individuals, how could one feel empathy? Maybe the German people remember World War II and remember how difficult it was to rebuild a country and trust.

The morning as usual came too quick, and, yes, George, you have to shave before going to school, I thought, *looking out and wondering how cold it was going to be. It's still winter, even here in Germany.*

I met some guys walking out of my apartment speaking German with one another. I thought, *If these guys were from this town, they would not live in this apartment.*

Three of them spoke English with me. *Yes, they lived here all year, but because Angela came for me last year, I had not noticed them walking to school. Here's my chance to learn German,* I thought, *which also was my first class.* I had not used the little I had learned the previous semester; therefore, I kept on speaking English of fear I might make a fool of myself.

Peterson was nowhere to be seen, just some young girls chatting away in English. But after a while, the class filled up, and Mr. Peterson introduced himself as we all did to one another. So it went with all classes.

School had begun, one day, one week, after another. David could not come because Mother broke her hip, and he did not want to leave her. I understood and was grateful for having a thoughtful brother.

At the Easter weekend break, I had time to visit the center for a checkup. Dr. Kopp invited the group—Jim my physical therapist and Dr. Philips my psychologist—who helped and encouraged me to walk again.

I remember Dr. Kopp saying to me, "I love these men and want to bring them back to a normal life as normal as life can be."

I remember how angry and disillusioned I was at that time, a nonbeliever of all that was told to me. I felt depressed and hopeless. *It was just a year ago, and here I am walking and preparing to live that normal life that Dr. Kopp promised.*

Surrounded by wonderful people and with renewed hope in my heart, I lived and worked myself through school. "Keep it up, George," was all I was told. Dr. Philips asked on the way out if I had met a lady friend as yet. "No time," I said, shaking my head, wondering why that would interest her.

It's time to see my buddy Jess for a beer and a hamburger.

"I am happy to see you, my George," he shouted across the bar. "Come sit for a spell." After a hearty greeting, he said, "I have good news. I am leaving this hamburger job and soon to start my new job as an accountant, hoping to get married by the end of the year."

"That is great news, congratulations. Maybe that gives me a chance. I am looking for a summer job. You think I could do what you do?"

"Sure, turning burgers? There is nothing to it, George. Let's see, a summer job that would work. That is two months as yet?"

"You know, I could do weekends even now while you are still around. Maybe there is someone who can hold on to work on the weekdays until summer, Jess."

"I will see what I can do, George. Leave it to me. Let's toast to success with a beer. The burgers are coming up shortly."

While Jess was finishing the burgers, I reminisced about my luck. The German family had remained true to me, and Ms. Molly had a basket with food to take home for the week. Angela visits me once, sometimes twice, during the week at school. Maybe, just maybe, a summer job would keep me busy and help save money for a car.

"How great is that? After summer, I have one more year to go. The burgers taste great as usual. You know, Jess. I feel I am a lucky man. It seems everything falls into place. And I am happy for you, Jess, and your success. I am sure you and Erna will have a great life together. Are you planning to have children?"

"George, let us get married first."

While walking to my apartment, my thoughts turned to Ann.

Will she call back, or will she stay away? Because I am—am I really in love with this woman, or is it a sentimental emotion of mine? I mean, George, you have not even met her, and the little bits of what Joe said about her were insignificant. What is love anyway?

The word *love* is used so frequently. One listens to music or reads cards; the word *love* seems to come up in language and culture anywhere. *Angela's attention toward me, is it love she feels for me, or is it a Christian duty that she learned and uses in her daily lifestyle? Well, the rest of the family is very good to me also. All the attention that I receive as a stranger is some kind of love,* I admitted to myself.

Yet it is unlike the love I felt when I listened to Ann's voice. I remembered when I hung up the phone, I named this new revelation *love*, and I felt that way whenever I thought about her. It's a different kind of love. I wondered with whom I could discuss this matter.

Angela is a levelheaded person. Jess is a buddy of mine. I wondered whether or not I could talk with Dr. Philips. *I don't even know if she is married, but one does not have to be married to be in love.* I passed the chapel going home and sat for a spell. *My place where I can unruffle my thoughts.*

Vivian shook my shoulders from behind and said, "Is that really you, George? How is life treating you?"

"What can I tell you, Vivian? I am happy to see you."

"The chapel is where I come just for a few minutes before I start my nightshift," she said. "So have you fallen in love as yet?" she asked, smiling at me.

"Funny that you mention it, Vivian. I believe I have and don't know what or how to handle myself."

She burst out laughing. "Wait a minute, dear, not so fast. I was just kidding, but you seem to be serious, George."

"Well, it is a long story and I don't know if it's love, but I've never felt this way."

"George"—she motioned her hands at me to stop talking—"I have a day off on Tuesday, if you want to discuss your feelings. I will meet you at McDonald's after school. I've got to go in a few minutes to relieve the day crew."

"It's a deal, Vivian." I sat and contemplated the love between Ann and me—two people journeying together, each one knows and understands the needs of the other.

No, George! I am hungry, very hungry for physical affection. Ann, if you were here, I would make passionate love to you. There I said it, right there in the chapel. I felt dazed with emotion and longing for physical love as I walked home. There was no message on the phone.

What a bummer, but maybe it was for the best. Who knows what damage I could make by saying what I felt if Ann had called? Easter Monday, I could call her just to hear her voice. It might calm me, never mind, concentrate on school in the morning.

Amazing how quickly the brain becomes lazy. It was just a weekend of not studying, and I had a tough time getting my brain going. *But, George, on with the show, if you want to build that new life with Ann.*

Weeks flew by. May came and went, but no phone calls from Ann or Angela. Although, I saw Angela every weekend, she used to call during the week just to say hello.

Did she find someone to love? It would be very natural, such a good-looking and smart woman. Well, George? I disliked gloomy thoughts like that. *Would she still pick me up to go to church? Would I lose her friendship? I had not heard from Ann either. Last time we spoke, she was still mourning her husband, but she could be mourning and still see someone, if the opportunity came. I need to know.*

The time was right; it was noon in Kansas City.

"George," she shouted, "I had given up on your promise to call. Are you OK?"

"Oh, Ann, I thought that you were going to call me, and I waited and waited, thinking, 'Well, maybe Ann found someone with whom to make a new life.'"

I heard her laugh and say, "I thought the very same thing about you, George." Feeling better already, the gloom left me, and I reconnected with my dream.

"Well, dear, I have no time for anything but study and keep my grades up. I want to be sure that when that someone comes along, I can provide a good life for her."

After some moments of quiet, I wondered what kind of effect my words would have on Ann.

"Is there someone you are thinking about, George?" she asked.

I wanted to say it, yet I did not have the nerve. She went on to ask whether or not I liked to study and whether or not I still believed nursing was the right profession for me. I told her about the psychology and anatomy classes and that I have learned to speak a little German outside the classroom. I was losing my fear of folks not understanding.

"You know, Ann, people are so very nice in this town. I like living here."

"I wish I could experience it," she said.

"So tell me, Ann, what are you doing? Are you working, or did you work before little Joe came along?"

"Yes, I was a secretary for a big computer company. They invited me to come back to work whenever I was ready."

"Very interesting. Will that be soon—I mean, going back to work?" I asked.

"I have been thinking about it, George, but I think I will enjoy my baby for a little while longer. By the way, do you know of Apple Computer, George? You know, they are building a very modern new facility in Germany."

"You don't say, Ann. You know in what city?"

"No, but I can find out."

"Would that be nice if Apple would send you to work?"

"Oh, George! That would be too good to be true."

"Would you really move to Germany and leave your family?"

"I am sure that Mom and Dad would understand and not stand in the way. Apple is a good company to work for. I do want to stay with them. It is my financial security."

"Ann, everything is possible with God," I said.

"So true, George. Sorry, I hear the baby he woke up from his nap."

"OK, Ann, call me soon and kiss little Joe for me."

"I will."

Great, I thought, *that was a lot of information to handle.* I felt such excitement. *Did I hear right? She was feeling lonely for me and waiting for a call from me. Why did I not tell her of my love for her? Too early, George. But on the other hand, I am wasting time.*

I went for a walk and ended up in the chapel. I let my fantasy go expanding my life's future with Ann as far as my imagination would go. *I let it happen, dreaming of having a home here, maybe a little pony for Joe, my son.* I liked being in this dreamlike state of happiness.

Apple Computer, I thought, *Ann surely will have a computer or phone. We could e-mail, we could exchange pictures, why didn't I ask her?*

I heard voices, and the lights came on. Father Paul sat down for a minute, saying, "Are you staying for mass?"

"Oh, I did not know there was mass. Yes, I will stay."

"Do you want me to mention something or someone special to pray for, George?"

I dared not say what I wanted more than anything, so I mentioned my buddies.

Father Paul looked at me, saying, "Is that all, George?"

Does he know what's on my mind? I don't think so, but if anybody does know, then it was the Almighty, and I do not have to mention it to a human being.

I wondered whether I should sit more in the front. I sat in the back when I sat in the wheelchair and remembered how little I believed that I ever would be able to walk and that was just a little while ago.

"Oh, God, chase away my disbelief and help me to strengthen faith in you to be steadfast and true." Another person played the organ but it was organ music, and we sang songs out of the hymnbooks. After the service, we greeted one another. I was touched by the friendliness. I did not know anybody, and yet it felt like a family meeting.

A bunch of people walked to the dining room, and I just followed along. I was invited to sit with some folks who had heard or read about me and asked about school and if I really would stay in Germany after finishing my program. Aside from such questions, it turned out to be a nice evening. I walked home in the gentle rain that kept falling all night.

On Sunday, Ms. Molly called early, "Do I pick you up, George?"

"Thank you," I said at the same time as she hung up. *Boy, what happened there? Was Ms. Molly upset? She did not give me time to ask about reasons for her to pick me up. Was Angela ill?*

As I was getting in the car, I asked about Angela.

"Oh, that kid is misbehaving lately. She went with a group of nurses on a trip to watch an outside concert tonight. She is not listening to anybody right now."

"Why should that not be OK, Ms. Molly?"

"Because she is not going with someone we know. That is why I am upset and worried."

"Would it have been OK if I had gone?" I asked, smiling.

"George," she said, looking at me kind of strange, "you are one of us. I would feel much better if you were there. I bet she did not even invite you."

"Well, Angela probably was thinking about my schoolwork," I said, trying to make an excuse and calm Oma Molly down. In my heart, I knew something was cooking as I noticed my stomach turning. That is why I did not hear from her during the week.

Angela does not have to tell you anything, George, but why am I so upset suddenly?

After lunch, I went with Joe to the field, cutting grass.

"The first cut," he said. "You know, it's a pleasure to drive this John Deere."

"I bet it is, Joe."

I wondered if the weather had been good in Apache. *I should call home anyway*, I thought and mentioned it to Joe.

"Let's just finish this row, and I will drive you home," he said. "Grandma might be having a nap. She has not been the same for a few days."

"I noticed, Joe. It's about Angela, isn't it?"

"Yes, you are right, George. I believe grandma wants you to get a move on. She likes you very much."

"I have nothing to offer her for a few more years, and on top of it all, I am a cripple—a cripple for the rest of my life," I said.

"I understand where you are coming from, George, but Grandma looks at life different. She knows what kind of upbringing you had. That is what counts, that is the investment that Grandma sees in you, George. Angela is a good woman. I know she likes you, George."

"Well, I like her too. She's been so good and patient with me. How could I not like—even love—her? But is it fair to her to tie us down on those grounds, Joe? My love for Angela, and I feel that her attention to me is more on a brother-sister level. I hope it will never end."

I imagined the house being quiet when David answered the phone, and I imagined how everything looked and felt on Sunday afternoons at home. I used to like Sunday afternoons. Mom usually had a nap, and when she woke, she would sit on the couch and watch David at the desk. But as soon as he said, "George, how are you?" Mom and my sister Margaret sounded their voices, "I want to talk with, George," and the house became alive. David was doing the finances. "My Sunday job," he said.

"I remember, brother."

I asked him if he was making hay as yet.

"Never mind, we want to know what you and Angela are doing."

"She went to a concert over the weekend."

"Without you?" David asked.

"Why do you sound so upset?" I asked.

"George, don't be so naïve. We believe she loves you, and Angela is a jewel and she would make the right wife for you."

I was holding the phone away from my ear because of the loud voices from Mom and Margaret.

Joe grabbed it, and he said, "We think so too, David. Hi, how are you?"

"These kids nowadays do not know what is good for them."

I was surprised.

While they were talking, I pulled two bottles of beer out of the fridge and handed one to Joe. I sat down and let the two wise ones make plans for Angela and me, thinking nobody knows my plan or Angela's plan for our future. We were very inexperienced about what is needed to prepare for living together a lifetime.

Maybe my concept of making a home with Ann and her son was naïve, but why do I feel so strongly about my capability of being a good father and husband? We will learn by living and working together how and what is best for us, and that is what Angela and I would be doing like all young married folks do.

"Here, George, talk to your sister. She wants to give you some advice," Joe said, handing me the phone.

"Oh boy," I said.

"Hi, George. How are you?"

"I am fine, Margaret."

"Still studying hard?"

"Yes, dear. Soon my first year is finished. I hope that I can work during the summer.

"Is your German that good, already?"

"I have not even been hired, but a friend of mine believes he could persuade his boss."

"Good luck, dear, and your love life? How is your love life, George?"

"I have no time, Margaret. Until I can afford and share a life with someone."

"You are smart, little brother. I pray that the right woman comes around soon."

"Thanks, big sister, I love you."

I listened to Mom patiently as she hummed about how wonderful Angela was to me when I was in need. "You know we all want the best for you, George."

"Thanks, Mom."

Hanging up the phone, Joe said, "Everybody loves George."

"Sometimes it feels like they all feel sorry for me, and I don't like it, Joe."

We drank our beer in silence.

"What about you, Joe, tell me, do you have someone other then your family to love?"

"I am a bachelor and want to stay that way," Joe said.

I looked at him. "So? Are you dating someone?"

"No, George, there is no woman in my life."

"How does that work out with your sexuality?"

"You know, George, I wanted to be a priest during my teens. Somehow, it did not work out. Dad had cancer and died. Mom needed someone to do the farm, and so I ended up doing the fields, and this life agrees with me. I love it. Somehow, I do not feel the need of being sexually involved with one woman, and I must say, I feel quite comfortable with my celibacy."

"Is it a curse or a blessing?"

"In my case, it is a blessing."

"Don't you believe in the human need for affection, the touch and the kiss and whatever follows, Joe?"

"Yes, I do believe in sexuality, but each person needs to find out what satisfies his or her hunger. I am very happy living here on the farm."

That did not make sense to me at all, but so what. Who am I?

Joe, looking at me agreeably, said, "I understand, George. We are all made different."

"Anyway, Joe, I think we use the phrase 'I love you' far to often in our speech, in music, lyrics, and poems."

"Hold on, son, I think we do not say it often enough, George. There are so many kinds of love. We humans are starving for love and attention. You spoke of being homesick when you were in the field. Well, that is, you were missing–the love of your families and familiar surroundings. That, I believe, is the universal problem in this world.

"Greed of man has robbed society of the simple logic of the heart and soul. We are bombarded with fear that makes us feel insecure and isolated. We try to surround ourselves with things that are relentlessly offered to us, believing that it makes us feel safe. The wanting seems never enough.

"Folks have to work longer hours to get back to that secure feeling of family ties, thereby getting further away from family and the feeling of being loved, too tired for the things that have been the best medicine, like affection and love. Like Sunday dinners with family, coming together for birthdays or other events, that gave old and young a feeling of belonging. We are doing it all ourselves, George, being dragged into a gully of becoming a loveless, insensitive, and lonely society."

After a long spell of quiet time, Joe said, "What you are looking for, George, is the kind of love you build a life with and have children. I think that is grand. You find her, or she will find you. Have faith. You are young.

"My advice to you is, live a little and maybe love a little before you settle down because once you have said 'I do,' it can be a very long and tedious life. There are ups and downs you may like or not." Joe looked at me.

I finished the sentence by saying, "It seems easier when you have the partner you love."

He got up. "Thanks for the beer. See you next Sunday, George. In the meantime, enjoy life a little, love a little, before settling down."

Closing the door behind Joe, I thought, *I had heard that before. Am I afraid to step out? Sure, I have buddies triumphantly boasting of this and that. I do not care for that kind of crude talk, and I usually walk away. Yeah, yeah, I could hear some guys snicker behind me. It does not bother me. Girls seem to like me, and I like their company, but that's as far as my affairs go.*

Since I heard Ann's voice, life changed. Some force I don't know had happened. Did it have something to do with my buddy Joe, Ann's husband?

"Ann, Ann dear, I need to see you. I need to feel you. I need to know you. I am madly in love with you and want to share my passion with you. Another year is not so hard, George, I can do this," I said these worlds out loud for me to really believe.

And so another weekend passed by.

CHAPTER 31

*A*ngela was waiting in my apartment when I came home. Having finished my last test in German, I was still feeling confident from the compliment I received from the teacher. I greeted her in German. She jumped up excitedly and told me how great I sounded and congratulated me in German with a hug and a kiss on my cheek. I pulled out a beer from the fridge and a glass for her.

We sat for a while, and then she asked, "What now, George?"

Looking at her, I said, "I don't really know. I have not made up my mind whether I should attend summer school or find a paying job."

"Why don't you become a nurse's aide? They don't pay much, but it will teach you a lot and you might be able to work weekends during your last semester," she said.

"Is there a class during summer?" I asked.

"Yes, it usually begins a week after school ends. That is what I did. It helped me get to know the staff and rules and regulations of how things work around here," Angela explained. "You have no idea how big this center is, George, and it is getting bigger. There are twelve hundred nurses working here. We have eight operating rooms, and they are in daily use."

I was getting excited and restless and wished it was Monday morning instead of Friday afternoon, too late to find out anything.

"Let's go for a burger at Jess's place, Angela."

I wonder if he had a chance to talk with the owner in behalf of me working there during the summer.

We trotted to McDonald's, Angela quietly beside me. I felt uneasy and guessed that she felt the same, but I did not want to open a conversation.

Jess shouted his friendly hello from afar. He came from behind the counter to greet us. "You two make a perfect couple. What is missing is a couple of kids."

"Woah, woah, wait a minute, aren't you rushing a little?" I said.

He sat with us and told us the news about beginning his job as a junior accountant close to where he lives with Emma, continuing, he said, "And, George, I am sorry about the job. The boss found someone that can work full-time."

Angela looked from Jess to me with her questioning look.

"Well, congratulations on your new job. I hope we will stay in touch, Jess," I said.

"Well, sure we will, George, I thought of you being my best man, or I just had a better idea, why don't we make it a double wedding?"

"Wait a minute. What are you two making up? I was only gone for a weekend."

"Angela, don't you see Jess is teasing you," I said, giving Jess a pleading look. I hoped that he would get me out of this pandemonium as quick as he got me in this mess.

Jess got up, saying, "Did you two come to eat? I will close early tonight. Emma's parents are treating us for dinner tonight."

I was trying to soften any misdirected thought Angela might have formed in her mind.

We ate while Jess cleaned up.

"By the way," Jess shouted over the counter, "we should have each other's phone number and addresses."

As usual, Angela, being a tad quicker than I, gave Jess her card.

"Mmm," he said, "fancy."

"Can I have one too?" I said, smiling at her.

"Here, you silly bugger," Angela said, smiling back at me.

We walked out together, waving at Emma, waiting for Jess in the car. Whatever followed, I knew that things had to be said to

Angela, but how to start to communicate in earnest was not easy for either one of us.

We walked in the gardens around the center, watching lovers necking and kissing, young families watching their children playing in a sandbox, and people coming and going.

Angela pulled on my arm, saying, "Let's sit here in the shade."

"Good idea, and then you tell me of your weekend with friends.

"So, you heard about that too. My grandma is still upset with me. It seems that I did a monstrous thing, George." Angela's head leaned against my shoulders, and her hands held on to my arm, pulling it toward her body. "Tell me, George, what do you think? I needed some vacation from the same old, same old. So I was asked if I wanted to come to a concert in the park. I said yes and was looking forward to being with folks I work with, having fun listening to a new band from the USA."

I teased her, sort of rocking a little, back and forth. "Poor little Angela. Oma does not want to let her beautiful granddaughter go.

"I can understand that."

"So tell me, dear, did you have fun?"

"Yes, I did have fun."

"George, can you keep a secret?"

Standing in front of me now, she said, "There is this intern. He told me he was interested in me and wanted to get to know me. You know, it's funny I've been keeping an eye on this guy for some time because I sort of like his mild manner with patience. I didn't tell him that, of course."

"Of course not," I said, making a face of total disgust.

Angela searched my eyes for approval, looking down at me as to say, "I dare you not to approve."

At this moment, I felt my little sister was asking her big brother for a big favour. It felt so very good. I stood up and hugged her and whispered into her ear, "It's wonderful, Angela. It's great."

After a while, we walked some more beside one another, each of us thinking, not wanting to disturb our own thoughts.

Funny, for sometime now, I was afraid of losing a dear friend by not loving her, but in actuality, I gained Angela's trust and love for hopefully a lifetime. How lucky is that, George? Again, I thought, *why Lord, why is it so hard to remember to give all my troubles to you to solve and trust that it will be done?*

I heard my mother talking, "Tell him, George."

It was dark before we walked to my apartment. I felt light in my heart, and my perception of Angela was that she felt elated and relieved.

Opening her car door, she turned around and, with her forefinger, pointed to her lips. "Our secret."

I nodded my head.

Walking inside, I thought, *Why should it be a secret? Everybody should rejoice for Angela. She is smart and able to identify the decent and the indecent individual. This man she is interested in, being an intern, he had to have brains, perseverance, and a deep desire to serve mankind. At least, that is what I had experienced in doctors and nurses here.*

It was easy to determine why men would seek Angela's attention. She is just a naturally beautiful individual; and after meeting her you feel her strength, inner poise, and basically a people lover. Yes, George, that is what describes Angela.

CHAPTER 32

*T*he weekend on the farm ended up more relaxed and positive than the beginning.

Driving me home, Angela asked me if she should tell her mother of her new friend.

I told her the story of how I waited and waited to tell my mom that I didn't want to go home to the USA.

"I told her how terrible I felt for days, having this secret. Believe me, Angela, I felt so relieved after I told her the reasons why I needed to stay. Mothers understand. I don't know why we all shouldn't be happy for you, that you found someone to love.

"Yes, the answer is yes."

"Tell your mom how and what you feel and let her run with it. She will take care of Grandma," I said.

"By the way, you tell me you were watching him for some time, what else do you know about him?"

"Not much. George, just of what other nurses tell me."

"What is his name, and is he from here?"

"His name is Allen. That is really all I know," Angela said, looking somewhat embarrassed. After a while, she continued saying, "We sat together on the bus home. He asked me if he could take me for lunch. I mentioned that I was working night shift. 'OK then, I arrange for someone to work on Thursday,' he said."

"Great, so if you like him still and got to know him a little better after lunch, then you let your heart tell you about the next step. Build a friendship and see where it will take you. But, Angela, do not hide anything from your mother. She knows what is going on. You would only hurt her feelings," I said.

"George, you are the greatest," she said, pulling on the corner of my sleeve and skipped to her car.

Somehow, my apartment looked empty; usually, I liked coming home. Yes, it is my home, but that night something was missing. *A plant would brighten it up, or some pictures from family will certainly give the room a little homely and lived-in look. Why do I feel lonely tonight?* I wondered.

What might Ann be doing? It was still early evening in Kansas. Taking off my prostheses, I debated whether or not I should call her.

George, what would you tell her? I could tell her… what, George, what? Hell, why can I not be honest and tell her what I am feeling like? "Ann, I feel alone tonight and in need to talk with someone," I could say that.

"Nothing wrong with that for beginners, George," I said out loud.

Should I spoil my dream?

I sat, nourishing my feelings of loneliness, when the phone rang.

"Hi, George," I heard Ann's voice say as I felt my emotions perking up."

"Well, Ann, what a coincidence. I was thinking of calling you."

"Little Joe is sleeping, and I was hoping you would be home and we could talk a while," she said.

"Sure, Ann, anytime. How are you?"

"Oh, I have been under the weather for a few days. It's been raining here, and that affects my moods, like I become lonely in the house. How about you, George? Working hard? What is on your mind?

"Well, you know school is out. I've been thinking about a job to make some money for a car, or whether or not I should learn to become a nursing aide and make some money that way."

"Tough decisions, George. It sounds to me a nursing course would be the better choice," she said. "You will figure it out, not to worry. By the way, do you have a computer, George?"

"Yes, I do. It's right here beside me."

231

"Can we FaceTime or even Skype?"

"I don't know, Ann, but here is my e-mail."

In no time, I read a note telling me how to Skype with Ann. It took me some time to find the word on the homepage.

Thinking that I was going to meet Joe's widow in just a few minutes made my head spin and a little frightened. I had envisioned her many times being good-looking and slim. *What if?*

In no time, I was looking at Ann on the computer, and Ann was looking at a man without legs. *A cripple.* I had forgotten my legs were standing in the corner. I was looking at my stumps. I quickly covered them with my arms and hand and cursing them at the same time.

Slowly lifting my eyes to see if Ann noticed my mortification, I watched her wiping tears.

"So sorry. I am so sorry, George." As our eyes met, she whispered, "George, I love you. I wish I could be with you at this moment."

Looking at Ann for a long time, her reddish curls stuck around a teary face, her dress loosely hanging around her body. *This woman had the guts to tell me she loves me. While I have been wrestling in my confused mind for so long, practicing how to tell her the same words.*

"I am so very sorry, George," she said again.

Here it comes, I thought, bracing myself.

Bursting out angrily, I said, "What are you sorry about, Ann, being too fast using the words 'I love you' before noticing my stumps? Is that what it is or feeling sorry for a cripple?"

We were still looking into each other's eyes; hers filled with tears while I knew mine where filled with sheer horror, anger, and frustration. I was on fire, feeling the ugly old hate burning in my gut, trying to conceal my body and mind from Ann, and amazed that the anger and fury was still with me.

For some time, no one spoke.

Wiping her tears she said, "George, I love you for who you are. You gave up your legs for your country. Yes, you are a hero. I don't know what's gotten into you. You have no reason for feeling sorry for yourself. You are alive and doing all the things you want to do. Just think about it, George.

"You have fought courageously to become well and are on the way to do good things for the country. How could anybody knowing all this about you not love a man as such?"

Realizing that I misunderstood what Ann was saying and getting my head out of the mud, I said, "Ann, you are a very loving soul, and I hope that I have the privilege of meeting you in person one day soon."

"I like that very much, George. Somehow, I feel a certain closeness to you, like having been friends for a long time."

"You know, Ann, I have the same feeling as soon as I heard your voice the first time."

"Great, George. Let's explore our inner selves and go from there. What do you think?"

"I am looking forward to that," I said.

I don't remember how we ended this conversation. I felt my world changing just as it did when I lost my legs. Recuperation had taken place as promised with good people around me believing. Only one year later, another moment of my life changed within minutes. This time, I felt doors opening for Ann and me. Fastening my prostheses over my kneecaps, I walked out, feeling disappointment and hopefulness.

I walked into the chapel and sat for a while.

Just a little more than a year ago, I sat here in a wheelchair, hating every body. I was suicidal. If my mother had not been there, I would have done damage to people around me and myself. Medical staff had faith and patience with me and in me.

Little by little, I was given bits and pieces of opportunities like staying in Germany to be close to my buddies, being able to choose how to become financially stable, going to school, and being as close to men and women by helping each and every one perform life as normally as they wish.

All these were promised to me. All I had to be was, perseverant and believing. Yes, I believe I will become the man that I hoped to become when I signed in the army. In the mean time I am living with the hope of a future with Ann as my wife; and little Joe as my son.

LANDSTUHL

*L*andstuhl Regional hospital is a military hospital located in Kaiserslautern a town in the German state of Rheinland-Pfalz. It is the largest military hospital in Europe; also called "the German Front in the Iraq War". Every day planes land at Ram stein airbase with severely insured US soldiers from Iraq where lives are saved, limbs amputated, and gunshot wounds patched up. The Iraq war front.-

A constant stream of grey C-17 cargo planes land and take off from the military base. These busy runways are kept free for planes moving men and material as quickly as possible.

The planes flying in from Iraq with severely wounded men and women have their own runway ending close to the emergency door were the wounded soldiers are being unloaded from a stretcher and taking care of immediately. Up to 25 soldiers are admitted daily mostly direct from the field. Doctors, nurses, liaison, and a chaplain are prepared 24 hours to admit these broken men at the entree of emergency. The chaplain greets each victim awake or in a coma with the soothing words "You are safe now, you are in Germany.

Iraq and Afghanistan aren't the only war zones supplying the hospital with patients. Landstuhl is the central medical facility for US forces in Europe and is responsible for the US military command that encompasses about half of US troops around the world.

All proceeds will be sent to: The War Amps 1 May brook Drive Toronto, on, M1V 5Ka

The philosophy of the organisation is amputees helping amputees. It is a not for profit corporation Act, registered as a charitable organisation with the Canada Revenue Agency. This mission was founded by Veterans returning from the first World War and remains very active in giving financial help for their artificial limbs, encouraging child amputees to develop a positive approach to amputation through comprehensive programs including tools for future independence.

ABOUT THE AUTHOR

*L*isa Sontgerath is also the author of her journal. Becoming a nurse and various articles. After her husband passed away and children married Lisa found a new goal and became a certified FAA flight instructor; challenging a men's world of graduating from commercial, instrument and finally instructor license teaching in Palm Springs area. Lisa lives in Bobcaygeon a beautiful village surrounded by lakes together with her husband Eric Kloepfer opening new doors finding new goal of helping humanity (maybe children) of becoming and fulfilling their dreams.

All we need is LOVE